SULTANS OF SLEAZE

Other books by Joyce Nelson

The Perfect Machine:
TV in the Nuclear Age

The Colonized Eye:
Rethinking the Grierson Legend

SULTANS

Public Relations and the Media

OF SLEAZE

JOYCE NELSON

Common Courage Press   Monroe, Maine

© Joyce Nelson 1989
First published by Between the Lines, Toronto, Ontario Canada
Cover illustration by Richard Slye
Cover design by Goodness Graphics
Typeset by Ann Phelps / Coach House Press

This edition not for sale outside the United States.

Library of Congress Cataloging-in-Publication Data
Nelson, Joyce.
Sultans of sleaze : public relations and the media / Joyce Nelson.
p. cm.
Includes bibliographical references.
1-56751-003-5. -- ISBN 1-56751-002-7 (pbk.)
1. Mass media--Economic aspects. 2. Public relations. 3. Publicity.
I. Title.
P96.E25N45 1992
338.4'730223-dc20
92-24850

Common Courage Press
Box 702
Monroe, ME 04951 U.S.A.
207-525-0900

In memory of all the disappeared

We are the most illusioned people on earth. Yet we dare not become disillusioned, because our illusions are the very house in which we live.

DANIEL J. BOORSTIN, The Image

Perhaps this is an obvious point, but the democratic postulate is that the media are independent and committed to discovering and reporting the truth, and that they do not merely reflect the world as powerful groups wish it to be perceived. Leaders of the media claim that their news choices rest on unbiased professional and objective criteria, and that they have support for this contention in the intellectual community. If, however, the powerful are able to fix the premises of discourse, to decide what the general populace is allowed to see, hear, and think about, and to 'manage' public opinion by regular propaganda campaigns, the standard view of how the system works is at serious odds with reality.

EDWARD S. HERMAN AND NOAM CHOMSKY,
Manufacturing Consent

Table of Contents

Foreword
by Richard Slye

THE ILLUSTRATION ON the front cover of this book is a photo-montage, which means that it is a documentary snapshot of our times. It is also a still-frame of the Great North American movie that never ends, in which our existence as characters presupposes that we act from within a fiction to get a glimpse of what is left of reality.

Photomontage is an assemblage. Or rather, it is a re-assemblage of photographs that are themselves assemblages. When the German inventor of photomontage, John Heartfield, began cutting up and pasting together the newsphotos and symbols of Nazi celebrities in the 1920s, he inaugurated a new practice from a terrible recognition: Fascism would succeed by constructing itself as an Image and that Image would be as important as tanks, perhaps even more important. The manufacture of this image of invincibility, of inevitable triumph, rested on two prior conditions: first, the public's fatal confusion of photography with reality; and second, the regime's grasp of the truth, which was the opposite – that nothing is more amenable to manipulation than what poses as documentary. Photography becomes the construction of the real for those whose reality is photography.

In the intervening decades, with the advent of television and video, the power to create secondary realities and present them as documentary has grown exponentially. The photographic (including the video) is still the construction of the real within a society that equates the image with what the image purports to represent. The word explains itself: re-present. After fifty years of interminable advertising, which has annexed to its colossal machinery every component of our civilization, including the family, politics, religion, values, history, love, and death, it is no surprise that the culture itself has become a commodified, flickering spectre while the lived experience of our common history is actual only as it appears a second time; re-presentation validates reality.

As you read this, the image-banks of advertising executives and their friends in public relations continue to pour out their daily tonnage of technicolour garbage, linking politics to perfume, celebrities to sausage, reducing the complex to the level of slogan, and jamming what is left of the air-waves with cartoons of reality. The ludicrous and the grotesque are categories of belated recognition of our common reality. That is why we smile and shake our heads knowingly at the outrageous, before locking the doors and stepping out into the collage of our cities, onto the fantasies of our streets.

George Bush as Dick Tracy? Who else but the tough-talking ex-CIA chief would be manufactured as the cop who cracks down on crack? And history's most secularized pope has for a decade been the West's Superman-at-large. The artist, when faced with this culture of images, deconstructs imagery with the hopes of getting down to what they are really about.

Similarly, Joyce Nelson in this book deconstructs the political / corporate framework in which these images are articulated and composed: the political and corporate background of this circus of deception. She explains how much of what we think we know about the world is concocted in big-city boardrooms by a public-relations industry that constitutes a clear and present danger to our collective future. This is a *real* horror story, thicker by far with the miasma of rot and evil than any Stephen King novel you can find. Here are werewolves in three-piece suits, vampires who appear as Responsible Leaders, and assorted ghouls whose graveyard diggings are transformed into seductive Edens (or golf-courses, at least). The Sultans of Sleaze. Exactly.

Acknowledgements

THIS BOOK HAD its beginning in a radio documentary series called "The Selling of Companies and Countries" which I did for CBC Radio's "Ideas" in 1981-82. The current situation in 1989 seems an appropriate occasion for a text devoted to the subject of the public-relations industry.

I want here to acknowledge my indebtedness to Geraldine Sherman, former executive producer of "Ideas", who provided a seven-year-long working relationship that was both felicitous and formative for me. Also, without a CBC press pass I would probably not have gained access to a number of people whose words are quoted in this text. Although the Public Relations Society of America did, in 1981, call for better PR for PR....

Other portions of this work appeared in somewhat different form in *Fuse* and *The Canadian Forum*.

I am also grateful to Robert Clarke, who edited the manuscript, and to the Between The Lines collective who made its publication possible, especially member Jamie Swift who made several useful suggestions during the rewrite. As well, I want to thank the people of Ontario, without whose financial assistance through the Ontario Arts Council the text would have been far more difficult to complete.

I

Introduction: The Image Brokers

IN 1984 THE U.S. activist group Action for Corporate Account-ability suspended its international boycott of Nestlé products. After years of stubborn resistance the giant food multinational had finally agreed to follow World Health Organization guidelines regarding the marketing of infant formula worldwide. The turnaround was short-lived: in October of 1988 Action announced that Nestlé was once again distributing free formula to Third World clinics and hospitals, encouraging mothers to forgo breastfeeding and instead rely on the marketed formula – a practice directly linked to malnutrition and high Third World infant-mortality rates.

Shortly after Action's call for a renewed boycott of the corporation's many products (including Nescafe, Taster's Choice, Nestea, Nestlé candy bars, Carnation, Libby's canned foods, and Stouffer's frozen dinners), Nestlé hired an independent PR firm, Ogilvy & Mather Public Relations, to advise on corporate strategy in trying times. Ogilvy & Mather's confidential report, "Pro-active Neutralization: Nestlé Recommendations Regarding the Infant For-mula Boycott", advised a strategy of "neutralizing or defusing the issue by working quietly with key interest groups" and "building relationships with individuals and groups that share Nestlé's inter-ests, in order to cultivate institutional allies".[1]

The goal of "pro-active neutralization" necessarily depended on initiating "an early-warning system through which Nestlé gains awareness of actions planned and is equipped to take appropriate pro-active or reactive steps". As the report explained, this means "grass-roots monitoring ... for evidence that opposition is spreading to previously inactive areas" and "utilization of formal and informal

13

networks that we routinely maintain with major national organizations – especially consumer and women's groups, organized labor, and health care organizations".

Besides engaging in such forms of counter-intelligence gathering, Ogilvy & Mather recommended that Nestlé be careful of media relations:

> As always, the media have the potential to exacerbate the issue, create much greater awareness than desired, and continuously find negatives in either neutral or positive news. In light of this, Ogilvy & Mather recommends that as a general rule Nestlé should be reactive regarding boycott materials and not initiate media communications. If the media ask questions or want a story, Nestlé representatives should judge and respond accordingly – not initiate. This avoids generating more awareness of the issue.

The confidential report also suggested that it would be helpful to "inoculate" Carnation, the Nestlé subsidiary that markets infant formula in the United States and Canada, against the effects of the boycott. This was to be done by establishing "a positive 'do good' public service campaign on behalf of Carnation" to show the company's social responsibility. Among the programs considered for such a campaign were the "Carnation Literacy Library" – rejected because it fell into a "crowded 'do good' area due to Barbara Bush's involvement"; "Carnation Combats Cocaine" – rejected as "too 'negative'"; "Carnation Racial Awareness Program" – rejected because of its "potential for media criticism regarding South African investments and boycott issue"; and "Carnation Care" – "a foster-care fund for HIV-infected children and infants".

Settling on "Carnation Care" as the recommended solution, Ogilvy & Mather's report then explained the benefits of this particular image campaign: it "addresses 'Public Enemy No. 1'"; it is a "grass-roots operation that cannot be perceived as 'buying the public's love or acceptance'"; it "builds strong relations with local communities and organizations"; it would be "totally 'community help'-related, with no commercial support"; and it is "unrelated to the formula issue".

Unfortunately for Nestlé, Ogilvy & Mather's confidential report was leaked to the press in the spring of 1989. As a result, Nestlé stated that it would not be implementing the recommendations, which had themselves been effectively "neutralized" by such exposure.

□

In Jungian terms, corporations and governments put forward a "persona" meant to be accepted at face value. There are many ways of constructing that persona, but most of them have to do with the nature of spectacle and that complicated fetish of this century, public opinion. The need for an institutional persona can be traced to a corresponding "shadow" side of the institutional endeavour: everything that is intended to remain hidden, obscure, out of the public eye, closed to scrutiny.

The discrepancy between the acceptable public persona and the private hidden shadow of a corporation or government creates a very vulnerable gap. It is what business professor Prakesh Sethi, author of *Advocacy Advertising and Large Corporations*, refers to as "the legitimacy gap". Though he does not use Jungian terms (persona, shadow), Sethi recognizes that it is this gap that threatens the dominant corporate and governmental institutions of our society. If everyone accepts the persona as is, then there is no problem: business-as-usual may continue. But if the shadow-side of a corporation or government becomes exposed and generally known, then the legitimacy of that institution is threatened. The public may boycott it, call for more stringent legal regulation, or (in the case of a government) throw it out of office in the search for more legitimate leaders.

Obviously, this gap must be filled before it becomes the terrain of social change. Challenging the legitimacy of corporations and governments is nothing less than exposing their "shadows": revealing the ways in which their activities infringe upon our health and safety, our environment, contribute to our oppression or that of others, despite what all their persona-related activity would like us to believe.

The "legitimacy gap", then, is the arena in which alternative political activity and alternative public-relations efforts may grow. The gap between institutional persona and shadow is the fertile space for activities that threaten not just the persona but the larger structure of which it is a part. Not surprisingly, this legitimacy gap is also the playing-field of corporate and governmental public-relations efforts, more often called "communications".

As Sethi states, there are two major communications strategies for closing the discrepancy between persona and shadow or, in his terms, for closing the legitimacy gap:

> One is to change public expectations more in line with institutional performance. For example, if the public thinks the oil companies are making too much money, one of the ways oil companies could deal with that is to simply educate the public by demonstrating that they are not indeed making too much money. The gap would be narrowed because then the expectation and the performance would have been brought closer together. So you're changing public expectations to make them closer to the reality of corporate performance.[2]

The often-used "pie graphic" to illustrate how a company spends each cent of each dollar of profit is a typical strategy for educating the public on the supposed impoverishment of the corporate entity.

> Another way is to change the symbolism of corporate performance to meet public expectations. "Yes, we are making lots of money, but look what we are doing with that money: we are investing it in oil exploration, etc." This is changing the symbolism because you really haven't made any less or more profit than you were before. You're simply changing the public's perception of what that profit is. The corporate performance itself hasn't changed.

In our times, changing the symbolism of corporate performance is the preferred strategy. This is evident, for example, in the Ogilvy & Mather recommendation to Nestlé regarding the "Carnation Care" campaign. Besides "inoculating" the Carnation subsidiary against the effects of the boycott, such a campaign would have helped to balance the shadow-activity of the company in the Third World. No doubt, the "Carnation Care" option was selected in part because it proposed to help afflicted infants, saying in effect: "Yes, we stand indicted on Third World infant mortality, but look what we're doing for HIV-positive children and infants."

It is this kind of corporate and governmental schizophrenia that is used to co-opt opposition. We are expected to be grateful for whatever "image" moves a company makes towards behaving more responsibly, even though with its other hand it continues to engage in policies that are reprehensible. The co-opting that results is actually part of the first "communications" strategy mentioned by

Professor Sethi: changing the public expectations so they fall more in line with corporate performance; thus we are supposed to assume that a cosmetic step in the right direction is the most we can expect in terms of change.

But, as Sethi states, "If neither of these strategies works, then you really do try to change your performance to meet society's expectations." This last alternative is, of course, the least preferable option for the entity involved since the status quo works quite well for those in power. Indeed, there is an entire area of corporate PR called public affairs that is geared towards ensuring that governmental policy, regulation, and legislation will not be so stringent as to call for any drastic change in business performance or activity. The best example I can think of is the issue of acid rain.

Canadian and Scandinavian scientists have known about acid rain and its causes (coal-fired smokestack industries and auto emissions) for thirty years. Getting that news to the public, much less stopping its causes, has taken a phenomenal effort by environmentalists, because they have been blocked on every side by corporate lobbyists with billions to spend. As John Sawatsky writes in *The Insiders*, his book about the public-affairs side of the public-relations field, "Significantly, the fastest-growing area of corporate development in the United States and elsewhere in the world was not economics, law, labour relations, production, or marketing – but public affairs. All the signs indicated that lobbying and public-affairs consulting would remain a growth industry, on into the future."[3]

While this area of PR has mushroomed over the last fifteen years, it has been accompanied by those two communications strategies for closing the legitimacy gap. Changing our expectations about what is possible, and changing the symbolism surrounding corporate and governmental activity, have both gone into hyper-gear at the same time that corporate lobbying and public-affairs consulting behind closed doors have increased exponentially. As media critic Morris Wolfe has succinctly put it, "It is easier and less costly to change the way people think about reality than it is to change reality."[4]

The attempt to transform the way people think about reality, especially as it is carried on through media relations, is one focus of this text, which argues that the role of public-relations practice thoroughly scrambles our accepted notions of "the news", of freedom of the press, and of "free world" politics generally. The PR industry is so unexamined and hidden, and at the same time, paradoxically, so pervasive, that it is usually not even considered in any political analysis of current events, or in any serious discussion of the role of the media.

For example, one of the hallowed beliefs of our time is that mainstream media editors, producers, reporters, publishers, commentators, and so on are the "gatekeepers" of information, that is, they control what will be known and what will not be known by the public, and in what terms. While this belief ignores the significant question of media ownership and reliance on advertising to survive and flourish (a situation often entailing self-censorship), it also conveniently overlooks the significant role of the PR industry in setting the information agenda. As the case of the PR campaign for Argentina in the 1970s (chapter 2) makes clear, an effective and efficient PR company can skilfully help to determine what will be "news" on the international scene. In other words, behind the media gatekeepers is another whole level of information-gatekeepers who are skilled in that most modern of projects, media relations and the making of "reportable events".

□

What works at the international level also works at the national, the regional, and the local level. For months in advance of the opening of Toronto's Sky Dome (known in some circles as the Con Dome), the local media gave almost daily coverage to each new development in the construction's progress. And in the final week preceding the official opening of the controversial $500 million structure, media hype centred around the stirring "drama" of whether or not the Dome would be finished on time. Behind the hype was CMC Communications, the public-relations firm run by Ron Willoughby. It was pitiful to see the front-page headlines of Toronto's dailies, and the extensive radio and TV coverage by Toronto's electronic media, given over to this late-breaking "news" story. One piece of newspaper reportage informed us that the architect's concept for the Dome was that it be the female equivalent of the phallic CN Tower standing just alongside. This was, perhaps, a subtle way of implying how badly we'd all been screwed.

But, as a rapidly growing professional field, public relations is much more than media relations. PR practitioners, either as employees of corporate or governmental PR departments or as members of an independent PR firm, specialize in several key branches: labour relations (also called employee relations), product marketing support, financial relations, community relations, public affairs (sometimes called government relations and issues management) PR, and international relations. Each of these areas can also be subdivided into further specializations, with the result that an in-house PR department may have a staff in the hundreds.

For example, financial relations deals with the financial community, which is composed (at a local, national, and international level) of stockholders, prospective investors, security analysts, investment counsellors, the financial press, statistical services like Dunn and Bradstreet, investment companies, bank, trust, and investment counsellors, insurance companies that invest premiums, brokerage firms, and the financial vice-presidents and treasurers of other corporations, as well as trade associations, business roundtables, and ministers of finance. Each of these also constitutes a "public" that must be related to by a large corporation.

The power of the PR industry is demonstrated not only by its hegemonic manoeuvrings within and for every area of government and business, but also by its remarkable ability to function as a virtually invisible "grey eminence" behind the scenes, gliding in and out of troubled situations with the ease of a Cardinal Richelieu and the conscience of a mercenary. When a PR campaign is exposed – for example, the proposed campaign for Nestlé – it is the corporate client (Nestlé) that tends to receive the brunt of the criticism, while the independent PR firm under hire (in this case, Ogilvy & Mather) tends to be perceived as simply doing its job for its client in the most professional way. Obviously, both corporation and PR firm are fully implicated by the "sleaze factor" at work in the mind-set and the manoeuvrings. By reframing situations to foreground the activity of the PR profession, this text attempts to reveal the incredible power that profession and industry have in modern life.

Clearly, *Sultans of Sleaze* is a small book about a huge topic. The focus, however, challenges that undying belief of our time: that we live in an open society, made even more open by advances in communications, by the proliferation of mass media, and by an "information revolution" that makes us the most informed society in the history of the planet. This text argues quite the reverse: that "misinformation" and "disinformation" more accurately typify our times, that the role of the mainstream media as "conduits" for corporate and governmental public-relations efforts has, in fact, increased exponentially over the past twenty years, and that the PR information-gatekeepers manipulate both media and public through a wide range of strategies founded on image-politics. Sometimes that manipulation takes the form of a drought of information, as in Ogilvy & Mather's recommendation that Nestlé be reactive rather than pro-active in its media relations. At other times the chosen PR strategy is a flood of information, part of what could be called "the politics of infoglut" — a deluge of data, facts, messages, "news", which all help to maintain the illusion of "openness" while obscuring the activity that goes on behind closed doors in the centres of power.

Besides analysing the PR campaign conducted for Argentina during the reign of the generals, this text also examines the new media-relations strategies that resulted from the 1960s PR crisis surrounding business-as-usual; the rise of the pollsters and their influence in agenda-setting and "communications" strategies, including the free trade election in Canada in 1988; the role of international PR in the most recent twenty-year-long rip-off of the Third World by multinational corporations; and the 1980s "enterprise zone" approach that has been pitched in Britain and the United States and is being implemented in both. Canada's free trade deal is, for many, an unappetizing part of this new Multinational Free Lunch. Finally, this text examines the new "green" image that most corporations and governments are hastening to adopt, especially helped by the Brundtland Report. As the latest fashion in public-relations endeavours, this trend is spreading like a pesticide through the whole food-chain of the rhetorical diet.

These cases are, certainly, only a few of the highlights of an industry that has been, and remains, perhaps the most significant part of this century of triage: a century whose persona is "progress" but whose underside is the efficient "culling" of entire peoples and species deemed to be superfluous, unnecessary, and in the way of the expanding technological dynamo. Ensuring the "legitimacy" of that holocaustic agenda is a significant part of the mainstream public-relations profession.

2

The Time of the Hangman

A terrorist is not just someone with a gun or a bomb, but also someone who spreads ideas that are contrary to Western and Christian civilizations.

JORGE RAFAEL VIDELA, President of Argentina, 1976

THE MILITARY JUNTA seized power in Argentina by a coup d'état executed on March 24, 1976. That same day the Generals issued their first communiqué to the world, stating: "The action of the government will be characterized by the respect of the law within a framework of order and respect for human dignity." The following day, *The Globe and Mail* reported further clarification from the Generals: "To eradicate subversion, the junta says it plans to eliminate the causes that favor its proliferation." More to the point was a statement made by General Iberico Saint-Jean, though his words did not make the mainstream press at the time: "First we'll kill all the subversives. Then we'll kill the collaborators. Then the sympathizers. Then the undecided. And finally, we'll kill the indifferent."[1]

Within six months of the military coup, human-rights organizations within Argentina were stating that at least three thousand people had been kidnapped off the streets by military death-squads. Two months later, Amnesty International conducted an investigation and estimated that at least five thousand political prisoners were being held by a regime where "torture is widely and routinely practiced". Another five thousand people had been kidnapped and disappeared.[2]

During Videla's reign of terror, from March 1976 until March 1981, an estimated thirty-five thousand people were "disappeared" – a new category of punishment that means kidnapping people, getting rid of their bodies (often by dumping them by helicopter into the

Atlantic Ocean), and altering the official records to show that they never existed, therefore no crime had been committed. Countless thousands of others were imprisoned and tortured under a regime that hunted "terrorists" and "subversives" through a network of efficient death-squads made up of members of the military. "In this holy war, the victims disappear," Eduardo Galeano writes in *Century of the Wind*:

> Those not swallowed by the earth are devoured by fish at the bottom of rivers or the sea. Many have committed no greater crimes than appearing on a list of phone numbers. They march into nothingness, into the fog, into death, after torture in the barracks. "No one is innocent," says Monseñor Plaza, bishop of La Plata, and General Camp says it is right to liquidate a hundred suspects if only five of them turn out to be guilty. Guilty of terrorism.[3]

Jacobo Timerman, former editor of the Buenos Aires daily newspaper *La Opinion*, was imprisoned and tortured for thirty months by the military, from April 1977 until his deportation in October 1979. Two years later, in October 1981, he told the Writer and Human Rights Conference sponsored by Amnesty International and held in Toronto: "In Argentina there was at that time probably one thousand guerrilla fighters when the Armed Forces took over in 1976. In five years they killed 35,000 people in this war against 'subversive terrorists'."[4]

Despite the efforts of human-rights organizations and some leftist journalists, the full reality of what was happening in Argentina during the reign of the Generals did not really penetrate the consciousness of the world until 1981. That was the year that Timerman's book *Prisoner Without a Name, Cell Without a Number* was published, giving a first-person account of imprisonment and torture in the military barracks and prisons of Buenos Aires. In other words, for five years the Argentine junta pulled off a public-relations coup that, in retrospect, must go down in the annals of "communications" as a horrific but classic example of international PR in action. Of course, the Videla government did have a little help in the matter.

Shortly after coming to power in 1976, the military junta hired one of the top independent PR firms in North America – Burson Marsteller – to improve its international image, especially for fostering foreign investment. In addition to the perceived threat of internal "subversive" activities, the new government faced an inflation rate running at between 400 and 800 per cent each year, a chronic balance of payments deficit, industrial stagnation, and widespread domestic unrest over wages and prices. Burson Marsteller, with offices in more than two dozen cities around the world (including Toronto), was a good choice to co-ordinate better international PR for the troubled country. Having already worked to improve the investment picture and international image of clients like Singapore, Romania, Spain, Sri Lanka, and Nigeria (during the Biafran war), the New York PR firm was skilled in handling delicate situations in troubled times.

Moreover, the company's president, Harold Burson, considered the PR mission for Argentina as something apart from the government's "political objectives". In autumn 1981, six months after the company's contract with Argentina had been completed, he told me: "Our representation of Argentina was unique in that we had no political involvement with Argentina whatsoever. Our mission for Argentina was fairly clear cut. We first were employed by the Ministry of the Economy. We did not work for the Foreign Office, we did not work for the President's office. We worked for the Minister of the Economy."[5]

Like many PR practitioners, Burson considers business to be an entirely apolitical sphere. "We will not undertake a purely political program for any country," he assured me. "We regard ourselves as working in the business sector for clear-cut business and economic objectives. So we had nothing to do with a lot of the things that one read in the paper about Argentina as regards human rights and other activities."

The Burson Marsteller mission for the Argentine Ministry of the Economy was, according to Burson, threefold: to "stimulate investment by foreign companies and corporations"; to "promote the sale of Argentine products" in the United States, Canada, and Western Europe; and "to introduce the Minister of the Economy and his subordinates, his high-ranking executives, to banking and other financial officials around the world so they could facilitate the borrowing process".

During 1976 the Videla government requested a 180-day moratorium on its international debt. It also presented the International Monetary Fund with a reconstruction program, resulting in a $300 million loan. As Noam Chomsky and Edward S. Herman wrote in 1979 in *The Washington Connection and Third World Fascism*: "The Economics Minister of Argentina, Jose Martinez de Hoz, is a free enterpriser perfectly in tune with the demands of international business, and a personal friend of David Rockefeller, who addressed a group of bankers in New York at a screening of a promotional film on Argentina" in 1977.[6] Rockefeller, chairman of the Chase Manhattan Bank and major stockholder in Exxon, told his audience of blue-chip investors: "I have the impression that finally Argentina has a regime which understands the private enterprise system.... Not since the Second World War has Argentina been presented with a combination of advantageous circumstances as it has now."[7]

Of the four hundred largest corporations in Argentina at the time, 57 per cent were branch plants of U.S., European, Japanese, or Canadian multinationals. A priority for both the Minister of the Economy and Burson Marsteller was to reassure them, as well as investors from the banking community, that the political climate of the country had been "stabilized" under the military junta. It was helpful, of course, that Jose Martinez de Hoz was also one of Argentina's largest landowners, director of a steel firm, two large insurance companies, two construction firms, Pan-American Airways, Western Telegraph Company, the utility Italo-Argentina de Electricidad, president of a finance house, and personal advisor to Exxon and Siemens.[8] By 1977, Rockefeller's impression about that "combination of advantageous circumstances" inspired U.S., Canadian, European, and Japanese banks to grant Argentina loans totalling $1 billion.

Meanwhile those "circumstances" were generating a somewhat different reality for Argentinians in 1977. The Argentine parliament had been closed since the coup, and opposition senators and deputies were being forced into exile and imprisonment, or sent to their deaths. As Peter Chippendale and Ed Harriman concluded in 1978, "Videla, 'moderate' though he may be, presides over one of the most bloody dictatorships in the world."[9] While the president was not among those junta members calling for a "final solution" to Argentina's half-million Jews, or condoning the bombing of synagogues, he nevertheless was devoted to eradicating "subversive terrorists" wherever they might be. His foreign minister, Admiral Cesar Guzzetti, said after addressing the UN:

My idea of subversion is that of left-wing terrorist organizations. Subversion or terrorism of the right is not the same thing. When the social body of the country has been contaminated by a disease that corrodes its entrails, it forms antibodies. These antibodies cannot be considered in the same way as microbes. As the government controls and destroys the guerrilla, the action of the antibody will disappear, as is already happening.[10]

This reference to military death-squads as antibodies helping to restore the "health" of the country was clever indeed. Amnesty International's dossiers and affidavits from people who somehow survived military abduction show just how anti-body those death-squads were. Their tortures included: "el submarino" – holding the person's head under water or excrement until near drowning; "la picana" – the electric prod applied to the most sensitive parts of the body; rape – sometimes by police dogs; tearing out toe-nails; and putting live rats to feed on fresh wounds.[11]

Galeano writes:

> It is the time of the hangman, but also of the conman and the conjuror. The generals order the country to shut up and obey, while the [finance] minister orders it to speculate and consume. Anyone who works is a sucker, anyone who protests, a corpse. To cut wages in half and reduce rebellious workers to nothing, the minister slips sweet silver bribes to the middle class, who fly to Miami and return loaded with mountains of gadgets and gimmickry. In the face of the daily massacre, people shrug their shoulders: "They must have done something. It's for a good reason." Or they whistle and look the other way: "Don't get involved."[12]

For the most part, the outside world could also look the other way, given much of the news issuing from Argentina. As Burson told me: "We had several people in Argentina who reported on the news, who did verifications, and we felt it was not only in Argentina's interests to get that kind of information disseminated, but we also feel it provided a service to the press in giving them news that was of value on its own. It was not 'puff-pieces', it was hard news copy." Given that public-relations specialty known as "news management", Burson maintains that his firm's involvement was entirely within the realm of those necessary "economic objectives". But to succeed with those objectives it was imperative to take certain steps, as a confidential document revealed.

□

In 1978 a copy of a report from Burson Marsteller to the Argentine government entitled "Improving the International Image of Argentina" was leaked to Amnesty International, which distributed it to various members of the press in Europe, Canada, and the United States. The report, written in autumn 1976, outlined the extensive public-relations campaign to be undertaken for the junta. Based on an eight-nation opinion poll conducted by Burson Marsteller, the goal of the campaign was "to generate a sensation of confidence in Argentina among the ranks of the target audiences in eight countries around the world, through projecting an aura of stability for the nation, its government and its economy".[13] The three target audiences mentioned in the report are:

> *Those who influence thinking,* which includes the press, government functionaries and educators. It is important to note here that we are not looking at the press as a conduit for transmitting specific messages, as is the usual case, but rather more as itself a target audience. *Those who influence investments,* which includes key persons in banks and commercial enterprises, investment counsellors, government functionaries concerned with international trade, businessmen and administrative consultants. *Those who influence travel,* which includes travel agents, travel writers, airline personnel and tour operators.

With regard to those "molders of public opinion – the press", the report lists *by name* specific reporters from fifty-two newspapers, news services, and magazines in five countries, all of them to be invited to visit Argentina. It also proposes to invite "well-known editors ... who participate in the determination of editorial policy", mentioning twenty-six targeted publications including (in the United States) *The New York Times, The Washington Post, The Wall Street Journal, Forbes, Fortune, Time, Newsweek;* (in England) *The Times, The Guardian, The Economist, The Financial Times, The Observer;* (in Canada) *The Financial Post, The Globe and Mail.* The report adds: "The Burson Marsteller representatives in each country have taken great care in the preparation of working press lists to maximize the chances of getting good coverage. With this in mind, we have mainly aimed at the business, travel and apolitical press. Where political writers are included, they are of conservative or moderate persuasions." The goal is "to build an ever-growing list of friendly press to invite to Argentina on a continuing basis".

Besides the creation of "school study guides", a TV special to be distributed to "the 120 major markets of the United States", co-ordination with embassy spokespersons, a program to position Argentina as "the 'in' vacation spot", and celebrity tours, the report recommends "communications training" for government officials in dealing with the media. This is said to be especially important because of "the Argentine problem":

> World opinion is being molded by accusations and reports that the Argentine government is not attempting to control the actions of the Right, that the police are involved in those actions, that no arrests have been made of Right-wing lawbreakers and that due process is not being observed with Leftist lawbreakers who are arrested. As a result, while the free world is predisposed to support the Argentine government in its intensive efforts to re-establish the political and economic stability of the nation, this support is being undermined, and may result in unfavorable consequences.

The section of the report entitled "Communications Implications of Terrorism" is worth quoting at length for its revelations about PR news management tactics and its "communications" advice:

> Those well-financed subversion campaigns of international origins can be confronted in two ways, both of basic and preponderant importance at this stage. One: the government should take steps to demonstrate and deal with all kinds of terrorism in the same way, and also halt any campaign of anti-Semitic or other nature, which denies civil liberties and human rights. This should be done without itself infringing on any basic civil liberties. This, of course, is easier said than done, but the need is clear. Two: an in-depth public relations effort such as the one being prepared, should be maintained in order to a) let the world know about the positive aspects of Argentine developments, supplying information which clearly reflects the presence of positive factors, that terrorism is not the only news from Argentina nor is it the major news; b) use the best professional communications skill to transmit those aspects of Argentine events, showing that the terrorist problem is being handled in a firm and just manner, with equal justice for all.

As we now know, the military death-squads did indeed "deal with all kinds of terrorism in the same way", applying the indiscriminate blow-torch and electric prod to flesh of every age and gender. The varieties of torture and execution that proliferated during the regime indicated that breaking the habit of "infringing on any basic civil liberties" was "of course, easier said than done".

Of necessity, the confidential report maintains the illusion that the "terrorism" in Argentina springs from "subversives" rather than from the military state itself. Nevertheless, there is a hint that the latter might be the case in most of the twelve specific recommendations near the end of the report, especially the following:

> In keeping with these general guidelines, we recommend the following: (1) heavy emphasis on economic information, showing the government is making all possible efforts to better the life of the average Argentine citizen, in this way depriving the subversives of one of their main propaganda points; (2) a strong campaign to communicate the fact that terrorism is not universal throughout the country. Those reports dealing with tourism possibilities, cultural themes, and other news that doesn't mention terrorism should be sought and distributed ... (7) Increase the amount of news released about terrorist activities in order to establish the absolute necessity of completely eliminating such activities from Argentine society. There is no better means of winning support than furnishing vivid evidence of guerrilla or terrorist brutality.

"We, in effect, conducted an economic business news service," Burson assured me, "and we reported on business activities in Argentina and disseminated that material to the press around the world. It was clearly labelled as information that was coming from us and from the Ministry of the Economy in Argentina." Following up on that extensive press list, "We invited members of the Western press and the Eastern press to Argentina. There were probably about five or six trips to Argentina where the press was invited to come down to Argentina to conduct their own inquiries." Those visits were highly structured, Burson recalled. "However, at our insistence there were at least one or two days where the press was free to move about the community in any way they wanted to whatsoever."

One Canadian reporter invited to participate in the press junkets was Alexander Craig, at the time a reporter for Southam News Service, which supplies news items to newspapers across Canada. Though not mentioned by name in the report, Craig was approached by the Toronto office of Burson Marsteller in September 1976, shortly after his article about a summer visit to Argentina appeared in Montreal's *The Gazette.* As Craig told me, "The fellow phoned from Toronto, saying 'We've seen your article on Argentina and we'd like to talk to you about our plan.' The plan was for a group, six or eight people from Canada, to go down and have two or three weeks, mostly in Buenos Aires." Craig told Burson Marsteller that if he went he wanted to have "total independence", including the opportunity to visit Cordoba where the CANDU reactor was being built. "I also felt I could use this opportunity to interview people such as Videla in Spanish – not a sort of prepared interview, but a free interview. Two or three weeks later, the Burson Marsteller representative phoned me and said there had been a change in plans and they just wanted economic specialists to go."[14]

One such specialist was John Van der Feyst, who reported back to *Canadian Business* (February 1977) after a special hour-long interview that General Videla gave to a group of visiting Canadian journalists:

> During almost a year of military rule, substantial results had been achieved which enabled [Videla] to look with optimism towards the future. "Some people call it a miracle," [said Videla] "but that it is not. It is merely the collective effort of workers and companies to sanitize the country and bring it back to economic health." When the word "terrorism" was mentioned, President Videla admitted that it still exists, but that the shoe is now on the other foot, with more subversive elements being killed than law enforcement authorities. People today support the new government efforts in denouncing the hiding places of the few terrorists that remain, he said. "But as you have seen yourselves, Argentina is no longer a battlefield."[15]

Such reportage indicates the degree to which a press conference or a pre-arranged interview laid on for a group of reporters can effectively establish the language and framework of what will then become "news". In this instance, Videla's emphases were all mirrored by the reporter's language: "substantial results", "achieved", "enabled", "optimism", "miracle", "economic health", "support", "few terrorists". Such language reflects the "positive" image, the "aura of stability", which was the desired goal of the Burson Marsteller PR campaign. As well, this reporter uncritically accepted the word "terrorism" to apply to "subversive elements" (Videla's definition), rather than to death-squads or the military itself.

A similar mirroring occurred in *The Financial Post* (December 11,

1976) in a report written by Frederic Wagniere after his trip to Buenos Aires:

> Credit can be given to the military for acting decisively. It wasted no time in cracking down on the terrorists and eradicating subversive elements from the ranks of the administration.... Decisiveness and orthodox economics allowed Martinez de Hoz to placate foreign creditors and negotiate a $1 billion medium-term international loan. The country could start thinking about living again instead of just surviving. Both President Videla and the Minister of the Interior say that terrorism is militarily no longer a problem, and that the government has the support of the people in its efforts to stamp out the terrorists.[16]

Supposedly, this kind of reporting is "objective" and contains no bias, though it is clearly evident that the language used reflects the very image desired by the whole PR effort. In other words, "objective" mainstream reporting can also be (in the succinct words of the Burson Marsteller report) "a conduit for transmitting specific messages".

Wagniere continued in a seemingly more critical vein, but again the terms were defined by the interviewee – Videla himself:

> Everyday, however, the newspapers carry accounts of gun battles between the army or the police and the terrorists. Few terrorists are taken prisoner because the army has the tendency to shoot first and ask questions later. Furthermore, there have undoubtedly been cases of Army officers taking the law into their own hands and going out gunning for terrorists or presumed terrorists. The army leadership frowns on it, but it's easy for a young officer, who may have suffered personally at the hands of the terrorists, to be tempted into lawlessness. The terrorists seem to be on the run.[17]

In handling the press, General Videla seems to have benefited from some of that "communications training" advised by Burson Marsteller in the confidential report.

In assessing mainstream press coverage of fascist Third World client-states of the United States generally, Chomsky and Herman note a number of media "devices that assure sympathetic treatment":

These include reliance on the juntas themselves for information; an acceptance of their verbal statements as to objectives and good intentions; a focus on alleged "improvements", on the "problems" faced by the juntas, on the infighting among the "moderates" and "hardliners", on the unfortunate lack of control by the moderates (at the top) over the hardliners (who kill people); and an avoidance of details on their gory practices and victims.[18]

Behind the issue of relying on "official sources" and PR-managed tactics like the press conference, the press tour, the pre-arranged interview, there is ultimately the deeper issue of language. As Timerman wrote in 1981 with reference to his newspaper La Opinion: "Every day it committed what in Argentina was construed as a capital sin: it used precise language to describe actual situations so that its articles were comprehensible and direct." Attacking both leftist and rightist extremists, as well as publishing names of the disappeared, the newspaper was also breaking some of the bounds of acceptable "objective" journalism. As Timerman puts it, "Newspapers write virtually in code, resorting to euphemisms and circumlocutions, speaking in a roundabout way, as do leaders, politicians, and intellectuals."[19] In breaking that code the newspaper, and Timerman himself, chose to place themselves at risk.

While members of the outside world's press corps were being treated to luxury motor-yacht trips up the River Plata with champagne on tap, Argentine journalists were getting a somewhat different treatment from their government. Timerman told his Toronto audience in 1981: "There was no censorship in those years in Argentina after the Armed Forces took over. No censorship. But nevertheless, according to the Commission of Families of Missing Journalists, one-hundred journalists have disappeared. So it was a kind of biological censorship."[20]

In 1977 the Argentine writer and investigative reporter Rodolfo Walsh circulated an open letter addressed to the military junta, documenting its crimes. The letter was published by the Argentine Commission for Human Rights. In it Walsh identified the major death-squad, the Triple A (Argentine Anti-Communist Alliance), as being made up of members of the three branches of the Armed Forces, and he wrote of the fifteen thousand people who had by then disappeared, the ten thousand political prisoners tortured routinely, the tens of thousands in exile, and of real wages reduced by 60 per cent. Meanwhile, he wrote, "the only beneficiaries of your economic strategy are the old cattle-growing oligarchy, the new oligarchy of speculators, and a select group of international companies such as ITT, Exxon, U.S. Steel and Siemens."[21] Galeano describes what happened to Walsh after he mailed his letter to the junta, with copies to foreign press agencies: "He is only steps from the post office when their bullets cut him down: and he is carried off wounded, not to be seen again. His naked words were scandalous where such fear reigns, dangerous while the great masked ball continues."[22]

At around the same time Timerman was undergoing the torture of "la picana", the electric prod, referred to as "being put through the machine". Later he wrote:

What does a man feel? The only thing that comes to mind is: They're ripping apart my flesh. But they didn't rip apart my flesh. Yes, I know that now. They didn't even leave marks. But I felt as if they were tearing my flesh. And what else? Nothing that I can think of. No other sensation? Not at that moment. But did they beat you? Yes, but it didn't hurt. When electric shocks are applied, all that a man feels is that they're ripping apart his flesh. And he howls. Afterwards, he doesn't feel the blows. Nor does he feel them the next day, when there's no electricity but only blows. The man spends days confined in a cell without windows, without light, either seated or lying down.[23]

In Timerman's case, the days stretched into months, while the great masked ball continued.

□

The junta's PR campaign found its *pièce de résistance* in 1978 in the form of that mass spectacle known as the World Soccer Cup. Staging the event to the tune of an outlay of $1.5 billion, the junta welcomed the opportunity to host the deluge of international media in attendance. As Burson Marsteller had advised in its report to the government, "Given the enormous coverage of the World Cup by the media, especially television, the event will offer Argentina a unique opportunity to present to the entire world what for many will be their first glimpse of the country, its people and its life-style."

According to Amnesty International and the London *Sunday Times Magazine* (May 7, 1978), a different agency handled the PR for the World Cup: West Nally Ltd., a Monte Carlo-based marketing consultants firm hired by the International Federation of Football Associations and the Argentine government. A well-televised event, the World Cup included an opening ceremony fully geared to the TV-eye: the release of hundreds of white doves flying out of their cages and up into the sky above the stadium. Given the hidden reality of the country at the time, it was a genuinely perverse moment of TV spectacle.

Alerted by the leaked PR report circulating in 1978, as well as the latest figures from Amnesty International regarding the imprisoned and the disappeared, many journalists in attendance at the World Cup attempted to get stories other than the actual games and the soccer-mania, but the attempt usually turned up little more than commentary about the obvious PR effort underway. Nevertheless, one of the best pieces of reportage in that vein was provided by Andrew Pollack for CBC Radio's "Sunday Morning". Referring to the Burson Marsteller PR campaign and the company's confidential report circulating among the press, Pollack told his listening audience:

> Journalists' organizations all over Europe have urged their members to keep their eyes open to what is happening outside the soccer stadiums. They point out that thirty journalists have been murdered and four hundred exiled since the military took power. The government has taken its own precautions against unfavourable coverage over the next three weeks. It has launched a poster campaign to persuade people to look happy for the thousands of important visitors. However, there seems to be little sign of this working.... More concretely, the authorities have issued press cards to no less than 3,000 so-called Argentine journalists. The local estimate is that at least half of them are police agents. They're also trying to make sure of a loyal crowd by handing out 5,000 tickets to each match to members of the security forces and their families.[24]

Making the best of a situation in which the only available story is the impossibility of getting the real story, Pollack provided a vivid encapsulation of the PR effort.

The World Cup 1978 situation also meant that, in many instances, sports reporters had to be political reporters as well. George Young of CBC Sports provided this summary:

> The World Cup began under the heaviest security ever afforded a single sporting event. Thousands of police were evident everywhere in

the streets of Buenos Aires and the other four cities where the games are being held. It was all a grim reminder that organizers were taking no chances in a country that over the last two years has had its share of political turmoil. President Videla in his speech referred to the fact that for the next month Argentina was being watched by the world, and he welcomes that. That's what this World Cup is all about. It has been a costly venture, but it's a public-relations vehicle.

Young ended his dispatch by interviewing a Buenos Aires-based correspondent for *The Financial Times* of London and *Time* magazine. In answer to Young's question, "The security that we see as we walk the streets, is that normal?" the correspondent answered, "Yes, there's probably a little less of it visible now than normal, I would say. The government is still fighting the remnants of the guerrilla groups and the government feels that the security which you see is absolutely necessary."[25]

Since opposition or dissent was punishable by imprisonment, torture, or death at the time, the likelihood of a reporter finding anyone in Buenos Aires willing to voice a perspective different from the one about "remnants of the guerrilla groups" was minimal; thus, Videla could make a speech welcoming the fact that Argentina was being "watched by the world" over the ensuing month. There was little chance that any member of the foreign press might penetrate the façade.

At the same time, former newspaper editor Jacobo Timerman had been moved to house-arrest. He was held captive in his own apartment, sharing the place with no less than eight policemen who left him with only the use of a small bedroom and a toilet (used as a kitchen). "The funny thing that happened," Timerman later recalled, was that during the last game of the championship, between the Dutch and the Argentinians, the policemen "had a big party and were shouting 'Argentina! Argentina!' and I was praying 'Holland, Holland'."[26] In assessing that other fierce competition underway at the time, Timerman says, "I would say that it was the Argentine government that won the battle of public opinion in the world with the championship soccer. They really won the public opinion of the world." The news management campaign was a success not only in "sanitizing" the image of the country, but also in making Argentina a virtual non-story. As Timerman states:

Time magazine, for instance, never had anything about Argentina. My friends in *Time* magazine didn't even report that I was arrested. They had only one cover story on Argentina and it was because of the soccer championship. And in the six or seven or eight pages full of columns about the championship, there were a few paragraphs saying that there are 20,000 missing people. And this was the first time that *Time* had anything about that.[27]

Two information data-banks reveal figures that are useful for assessing coverage of Argentina in 1978, the year of the World Cup and thus the year most likely to have generated the greatest press coverage about the country. *The Globe and Mail's* InfoGlobe indexes everything published by that newspaper since autumn 1977. The New York Times Service provides the InfoBank, which indexes virtually all news and editorial matter from the late city edition of *The New York Times*, as well as significant news items, articles, wire stories, and business news appearing in almost sixty other publications, including *The Chicago Tribune, The Christian Science Monitor, The Los Angeles Times, The Washington Post, Business Week, Fortune, The Wall Street Journal, Atlantic, Newsweek, Time,* and *U.S. News & World Report*.

Each data-bank can tell the user how many articles and news items appeared containing the word "Argentina" in a given year. This provides a rough idea of at least the quantity of coverage of the country, although the word may appear in an article devoted to world beef prices or the history of the tango. For the year 1978, InfoGlobe indicates that *The Globe and Mail* published 534 separate items containing the word "Argentina", while the *Times* InfoBank lists 444 such items for that year. So, to begin with, one Canadian newspaper published more articles and items mentioning Argentina in 1978 than almost sixty U.S. periodicals and newspapers combined.

Each of the data-banks further allows the user to refine the search for coverage figures by keying in other significant words to accompany the main word, "Argentina". Since soccer and the economy were the two main "positive topics" helping to maintain the acceptable façade of the Argentine junta, I asked each data-bank to indicate how many of those 1978 items also contained the word "soccer" (InfoGlobe: 119 items; InfoBank: 25 items) or "economy" (InfoGlobe: 22 items; InfoBank: 25 items).

For comparative purposes, I then keyed in significant words that suggest coverage of the hidden, or shadow-side of Argentina in 1978. Of those 534 *Globe and Mail* items containing the word "Argentina", 17 also contain the word "torture", 11 contain the word "disappeared", and 4 items contain the word "death-squads". For the 444 New York Times Service items mentioning "Argentina", 6 also contain the word "torture", 3 contain the word "disappeared", and 1 contains the combined word "death-squads".

Key Words	InfoGlobe	InfoBank
"Argentina"	534	444
and "soccer"	119	25
and "economy"	22	25
and "torture"	17	6
and "disappeared"	11	3
and "death-squads"	4	1

From such data at least two conclusions emerge. First, in 1978 one Canadian newspaper was significantly better at covering the shadow-side of the Argentine junta, the internal reality of the time of the hangman, than sixty major U.S. publications combined. Though even *The Globe and Mail*'s coverage of this aspect was minimal by comparison to its coverage of "positive" themes, nonetheless the figures are revealing. Second, the Canadian paper gave almost a quarter more coverage to the country than did its U.S. counterparts, indicating a greater recognition of the importance of Argentina as a news story at the time.

But then I compared the quantitative coverage figures with those of another country for the same year. I chose Sweden, one-third the population size of Argentina. For the year 1978 InfoGlobe indicates 747 items including the word "Sweden"; InfoBank lists 438 such items; thus, in these North American newspapers and periodicals in 1978, Sweden was at least mentioned more often than Argentina (InfoGlobe) or as often (InfoBank), although presumably nothing of comparable and horrific significance was happening there at the time.

Such low press coverage was by no means a public-relations failure. Instead, it was of benefit to the Argentine regime for its country and internal activities to be considered a relatively insignificant news story. Chomsky and Herman have provided insight into the notion of newsworthiness as it functions in the mainstream North American press. In *The Washington Connection and Third World Fascism* they write: "The trial of a single Soviet dissident, Anatol Shcharansky, received more newspaper space in 1978 than the several thousand official murders in Latin America during the same year, not to speak of the vast number of lesser events such as tortures and massive dispossession."[28] As Timerman told The Writer and Human Rights Conference, "I think that the world, as usual, deals with fascist countries in a different way than they deal with communist countries. I mean the Western democratic world. The Western world went to the Olympics in Germany in 1936, and the Western world went to the World Championship in Argentina in 1978, but many of the Western countries did not go to the Soviet Union, to Moscow for the Olympics [in 1980]. This is a double standard."[29] But it is a double standard made "necessary" by the relationship between Third World fascism and First World governments.

In 1979, for example, the election of Margaret Thatcher led to increased trade between Britain and the Argentine military. Ed Harriman writes in *Hack: Home Truths about Foreign News*: "Cecil Parkinson, chairman of the Conservative Party, had toured not just Argentina, but Chile and Uruguay as well shortly after Mrs. Thatcher came to office, looking for firm orders for Britain's recession-struck arms firms."[30] The result was a low-profile parade of a variety of Argentine generals visiting Britain's blue-chip armaments companies such as Rolls Royce, Westland Helicopters, Hawker Siddeley, BAC, Lucas Aerospace, and Short Brothers in Belfast. Whether or not the Burson Marsteller office in London was helping to facilitate the shopping trips is not known, but the activity would certainly fall within the parameters of that overall economic PR objective. The fact that the armaments would later be used in the Falklands War is one of those abiding paradoxes of our time.

Similarly, as Chomsky and Herman wrote in 1979, the U.S. government was not about to take too strong a stand with regard to the issue of human-rights violations:

The [Carter] administration has striven mightily to maintain the friendly relationship with the Argentine junta, with Secretary of State Vance making a special trip to Buenos Aires and with strenuous efforts devoted to preserving some flow of both "security assistance" and military training aid. The Pentagon, in the words of one high ranking officer, is trying to "maintain the special relationship we have with the Argentine Armed Forces."[31]

While some members of the U.S. Congress were quietly helping to secure the release of Timerman, other branches of government were engaged in business-as-usual.

□

Argentina during the time of the hangman provides an example of what Chomsky and Herman call "the consistent lesson of history". That lesson is that the United States and its allies in the over-developed world "will give massive support to the regimes of tortur-ers and gangsters that it imposes by force and subversion as long as they are successful in maintaining the kind of 'stability' that suits U.S. interests".[32] In 1979 President Jorge Rafael Videla received a letter from U.S. banker David Rockefeller. As quoted in Galeano's *Century of the Wind*, Rockefeller wrote:

> I am very grateful to you for taking time to receive me during my recent visit to Argentina. Not having been there for seven years, it was encouraging to see what progress your government has made during the past three years, both in controlling terrorism and strengthening the economy. I congratulate you on what you have achieved and wish you every success for the future.[33]

Since the goal of the Burson Marsteller PR campaign was to ensure that the country be perceived in the right circles as having achieved "stability", such a letter adequately confirmed the full success of the campaign.

To that "consistent lesson of history" we must add the least-known element in the whole equation: the public-relations special-ist. Even Chomsky, for all his extraordinary research into First World reporting on Third World subfascism, has not, to my knowl-edge, explored the role of public-relations firms in facilitating not only financial and inter-governmental relations, but also the whole image-making process vis-à-vis the media.

Most of the top independent PR firms take on a wide range of for-eign clients, especially governments wishing to improve their investment prospects. In this sense, Burson Marsteller's five-year public-relations campaign for Argentina was, and is, by no means atypical. When I asked Harold Burson if PR firms like his are in any way limited by the U.S. government, specifically by the State Department, he answered:

> We are not limited by the U.S. government in any way whatsoever other than to disclose for whom we are working, what our program for that foreign entity is, how much they are paying us. We must identify all the material that we release on behalf of a foreign government, or other foreign party from whom we are registered, and also we must provide copies to, not the State Department but the Department of Justice. As a matter of policy, we informally inquire of the State Department, of the Senate Foreign Relations Committee, of the White House, whether it would be in the interests of our government to represent a certain foreign government. We get informal responses which do not in any way govern whether or not we would accept. On the other hand, we have never undertaken an assignment which we felt would be inimical to the best interests of the United States.

At the same time that Burson Marsteller was representing its foreign client, another U.S. public-relations firm had taken on an equally difficult "assignment". Sometime in 1976 Anastasio Somoza, right-wing dictator of Nicaragua, hired the Washington PR firm Mackenzie McCheyne Inc. to improve its international image in the midst of rampant repression and slaughter by Somoza's national guard.[34] One of the two key target audiences for the campaign was the financial community, a "public" of international proportions best reached through the pages of the financial press. Using a commonplace PR tactic, the firm placed a two-page advertisement in *The Wall Street Journal* (May 31, 1977) with the heading "Nicaragua: An Investor's Dream Come True" and smaller copy which touted the dimensions of the dream:

> The subheadings give the flavor: "American Chamber of Commerce Invites Investment in Nicaragua", "A Country Where Foreign Capital Is Nurtured"; "Yanquis Feel at Home", "A Good Export Base", "Industrial Parks", "Great Opportunities", etc. Here the U.S. investor will find "a good investment climate", "stability, peace and a prospering economy", and will even be provided by the U.S. Chamber of Commerce with "a comprehensive guide for setting up business in Nicaragua, to share its experiences with others and to explain this

country's policies and practices in support of the Free Enterprise System".[35]

Whether or not such an ad helped to convince the financial community to further invest in Somoza's regime, it was part of reaching that other important target audience: the U.S. government. As Chippendale and Harriman wrote in 1978, referring to the success of the PR firm's government-relations strategy of the previous year: "Both the U.S. Senate and the House of Representatives voted to continue topping up the over twenty million dollars the U.S. government has spent on military aid to Somoza's security forces over the years. Nicaraguan National Guardsmen get their training in their 'counter-terror' methods from U.S. advisors at the School of the Americas in the Panama Canal Zone."[36]

The late 1970s were a boom-time for international PR specialists skilled at handling delicate situations. To the activities of Burson Marsteller and Mackenzie McCheyne Inc. we must add at least one other top U.S. public-relations firm engaged in image cleanup in dubious times and places: the Hannaford Company of Washington, D.C., hired by President Romeo Lucas García to help make Guatemala attractive.[37]

For several generations the country had (and has) been a political football of the United Fruit Company, Del Monte, and the CIA, as well as a host of other multinationals including Coca-Cola, Union Carbide, Dow Chemical, ITT, Colgate Palmolive, Eli Lilly, and Bristol-Meyers. Private death-squads have "disappeared" thousands of people over the years. Journalist Ed Harriman writes of his 1979 trip to Guatemala:

> The day I left Guatemala I had two calls to make. The first was to President Lucas' offices where his private secretary, an urbane officer, immaculately dressed and manicured, explained to me in an ornate ante-room that like Ireland, or England, or anywhere, Guatemala had its own level of violence and criminality. "You shouldn't over-exaggerate these things," he said. "And what about the Yorkshire Ripper? Doesn't every country have its own level of violence?" There seemed little point in drawing finer distinctions with him. "You are here," he set forth. "You can see there is freedom in every sense, freedom of expression, to work, to travel."[38]

But it wasn't long before the Guatemalan military found a more efficient answer to the tricky problem of media relations. As Julia Preston, associate editor of Pacific News Service, wrote in 1982: "The faster Guatemala spirals toward civil war, the less the country is reported on. For at least nine months, Guatemalan authorities have had a list at the Guatemala City airport of foreign journalists to be kept out." That list included *The New York Times*, *The Washington Post*, CBS News, and National Public Radio. As Preston writes:

> Rather than rely on the press for good notices, the government and private rightist associations have turned for an image lift to U.S. public-relations firms, including the Hannaford Company of Washington, D.C., of which presidential assistant Michael Deaver was a partner before he joined the Reagan administration.... Several of these firms monitor what is written, by whom, about Guatemala.... It is a truism that in U.S. foreign reporting, the State Department often makes the story.[39]

In 1981 I asked Cameron Smith, who was managing editor for *The Globe and Mail* at the time, how he could tell whether something coming over the wire services was, or was not, part of a "news management" campaign being conducted by a PR firm for a foreign government. "In large part," he answered, "you judge what comes in on the wires against what you're getting from your reporters. There may be a PR firm, for instance, acting on behalf of the American position in El Salvador. Let's say for the sake of argument," he continued, "that they did succeed in selling that story to Associated Press. You'd probably get a different story from *The New York Times*, from Reuters, maybe from UPI, from *The Times* of London, from our own reporter in Central America, from *Latin America*, which is a publication that has long dealt with Latin American topics, from other newspapers and journals, from freelancers.

"The chances," said Smith, "of that particular PR firm pulling off a PR coup in the sense that it is presenting a situation in a false light are not very good." But when I mentioned the example of Argentina, Smith immediately nodded. "Yes," he said, "the possibility can exist."[40]

It would be naive, however, to assume that governments, or the PR firms they hire, care particularly about the general public's opinion in these matters. As another international PR specialist explained, "These countries are not trying to attract investment from the general public." Andrew Weil, head of Warren Weil Public Relations Inc. in New York, told me, "What matters is what the *commercial* public will feel with regard to the stability of the government and the security of investment." In these terms, a well-executed public-relations campaign for a foreign government must demonstrate "that commitments made this year will be in effect ten years from now, that you can repatriate your money without heavy and excessive taxation, and that nationals of your country can work in this foreign country without being in any way penalized."[41]

The case of Argentina during the reign of the Generals shows that the way in which a host government goes about creating the necessary "favourable business climate" internally, vis-à-vis political dissent, is pretty much its own affair. Once the international community of high finance is convinced that "stability" has been achieved, the public-relations campaign is deemed a success. It helps, of course, if world opinion is reassured about things like human rights. And here another recommendation by Burson Marsteller to the Argentine junta is revealing. The confidential report states:

> When the time comes, an international commission should be invited to visit Argentina to investigate terrorism and the government program to bring it to a halt. (The government of Nigeria accepted a similar proposal of ours during the Biafran War, when the government was accused, by propagandists in Europe paid by Biafra, of generalized genocide. The commission reported that there was no basis in fact for the propaganda campaign).

Such findings would, of course, become part of the overall news management media strategy. As another international PR specialist bluntly states, "In this business, we have to be ahead of the news."[42]

3
Handling the Legitimacy Gap

Pseudo-events spawn other pseudo-events in progression. This is partly because every kind of pseudo-event (being planned) tends to become ritualized, with a protocol and a rigidity all its own.

DANIEL J. BOORSTIN

"BEING AHEAD OF the news," as the PR specialist would say, is, of course, a euphemism for creating the news, which has been one of the major areas of PR endeavour ever since Ivy Lee recognized, back in 1906, that there was a percentage to be made from disaster. In the early 1900s he had been hired by the Pennsylvania Railway as a consultant, advising on ways to improve business. When a major train accident took place on the main line near the town of Gap, Pennsylvania, Lee saw an opportunity in an otherwise dismal situation.

Traditionally, railways had always tried to suppress information about train accidents, fearing that widespread knowledge of, or reporting about, such incidents would be harmful to future business. But Lee was more in tune with the trends of the new century. He invented the "press release" (also called the news release), and issued the first ones as a way of handling the mishap. It was a major gamble on Lee's part, but he sensed (correctly) that the press would be grateful for the company's "openness" and assistance in getting out the news. He also recognized that the press release could help to determine how the event would be reported, and even potentially help to improve business rather than hinder it.

What the press release does is establish lines of control regarding information. It initiates the news-making process, and sets ideal boundaries around what is to be known by emphasizing some information and leaving out other information. An enterprising reporter can follow up a press release, asking further questions and seeking out other sources of information, but often, given the constraints of news deadlines, availability of alternative sources, and other factors, this isn't done. As well, for most of this century reporters have tended to be generalists, not specialists. Lee recognized that his helpful information could fill in the gaps of reporters' knowledge: in this instance, by incorporating into the news release information about the company's historical record or details about railway schedules and fares. Afterwards, other railways were forced to follow Ivy Lee's example or risk being perceived as suppressing the news.

The press release has remained a staple of public-relations newsmaking practice, with corporations, organizations, and governments generating a deluge of such releases every day. By the late 1940s there were estimates that as much as 50 per cent of the reported news in newspapers and on radio was based on press releases sent out by public-relations departments and firms.[1] The financial press has especially come to rely on the press release for its news. As recently as 1978 a poll conducted by Hill and Knowlton (the biggest independent PR firm in North America) revealed that financial news editors consider public-relations practitioners their "most important source" of news.[2]

In many ways the press release is part of the "politics of infoglut". It offers institutions a way to be seen as open and forthcoming about their activities. As John O'Connor, head of public relations for Ontario Hydro, puts it: "A few years ago, we were criticized for secrecy and withholding of information, so we've taken major steps to make sure that everything in this corporation is open to public view."[3] One of those steps has been a deluge of press releases, which has sometimes worked wonders for the corporation's legitimacy gap.

On August 20, 1981, for example, Ontario Hydro dumped heavy water containing 3500 curies of radioactive tritium into the Ottawa River – an accident involving more radioactive tritium than was sitting inside the crippled Three Mile Island reactor at the time. This nuclear "incident" got front-page coverage in The Globe and Mail, made the nightly TV news, and generated a fair amount of media commentary.

Then, just one week later, a peculiar item appeared in The Toronto Star. In reading it, one would never know that it referred to what was (until December 1988) the greatest release of radioactive tritium (8,000 curies) in the history of the CANDU nuclear power program.[4] The news item, in its entirety, was this:

> Armed with mops, pails and pumps, an Ontario Hydro crew has recovered 3,400 gallons of radioactive heavy water spilled at the Bruce Nuclear Plant Sunday morning. But the 360 gallons of special cooling water, which vaporized and escaped from the plant into the air, will cost Hydro nearly $450,000. Restoring the recovered water will raise the bill to about $1 million. Hydro spokesmen said yesterday the radioactive vapor which escaped through the plant's ventilating system produced no radiation exposure to employees or residents in nearby Kincardine. The spill caused by "human error", according to Hydro officials, sent 3,800 gallons of heavy water worth more than $4 million cascading out of a tank, through the reactor building and into the basement of the Number 2 reactor at the Bruce plant. The 850-megawatt reactor had already been shut down for routine maintenance and the heavy water was being drained from boilers into a holding tank.

The item has all the flavour of an Ontario Hydro press release: the opening sentence establishes the mental image of a cleanup crew with mops and pails, as though heavy water were no more dangerous than spilled dishwater. The rest of the item emphasizes the financial cost of the accident – less worrying than health and environmental hazards – and makes no mention of radioactive tritium at all.

According to Norm Rubin of Energy Probe, this is a good example of "a news item written with press release in hand", in this case referring to the largest spill that he knew of at that time but "one of the smallest nuclear stories ever written".[5] The "incident" got even less coverage in the The Globe and Mail. In terms of media relations, we can understand this reportage in the context of the previous week's extensive coverage of a smaller "incident". Following the glare of publicity with even more press releases was a useful strategy. As Ontario Hydro's O'Connor said at the time: "My basic feeling is that people are getting a little tired of hearing about nuclear power. So what happens from a newspaper perspective is that while it's new news, it's old news."[6] Moreover, the PR tactic also fits in with one of the prevailing conventions of news: that rectifying "misinformation" is not considered a news story. As Rubin states,

"The fact that Energy Probe says this is important on day two is not in itself newsworthy."[7]

Thus, Ivy Lee's strategy for that train wreck in 1906, the press release, reverberates down through the years for the handling of any disaster. As he recognized, what the public-relations practitioner must do is establish the framework for the event, the language by which it will be discussed and reported, and the emphasis to be maintained. Under Lee's guidance, the new field of PR (especially media relations) became a necessary feature of corporate business.

In 1914 Lee and William Lyon Mackenzie King went to work for the Rockefeller family in the United States, at a time when the repercussions following a massacre at Ludlow, Colorado, called for new strategies for corporate entities. Faced with public outrage and bad press surrounding the events at Ludlow, in which many striking miners and their families had been killed under fire by the National Guard, the Rockefeller family (major bond-holder in the Colorado mining properties) needed an immediate emergency image clean-up. As I have documented elsewhere, Ivy Lee and Mackenzie King together worked out a variety of PR tactics that were to give the emerging profession a great leap forward.[8]

They utilized the press tour – the first instance of a "goodwill trip" by an industrialist – in which Rockefeller Jr. (accompanied by an entourage of reporters) met the striking Colorado miners on their turf. Rockefeller's speeches to the miners, his attempts to good-naturedly swing a pick-axe in front of the mine face, his jovial lunches and parties for the miners, all provided forerunners to "the photo-opportunity" and worked to generate better press coverage for the controversial millionaire. Lee and Mackenzie King also arranged interview-opportunities and what must be seen as the prototype for the press conference, with Rockefeller Jr. coached in advance on how to handle hostile reporters. They set up what now would be called a "hospitality suite" in which Rockefeller Jr. courted labour leaders and union organizers. And Mackenzie King, highly skilled in such matters, coached Junior in advance of his appearance at government hearings to investigate the Ludlow disaster. The former Canadian labour minister also invented a new labour-relations policy for Rockefeller, including the formation, in effect, of a "company union".

Thus by 1915 the new profession of public relations was perfecting several of its branches: labour relations, government relations (now more often called "public affairs" PR), and media relations. On other necessary PR fronts – financial relations and international relations – Rockefeller had less to worry about. But it was especially in the area of media relations that Ivy Lee and Mackenzie King showed their brilliance. In their understanding of the new media age, these two had image-creation down pat, making the old "white-washers" look as outdated as the term.

□

It is probably fair to say that PR is as old as the papal succession, but as a specialized profession it is only within this century that PR has become an organized and formalized industry, growing in tandem with both multinational capital and mass media, each of which fundamentally helped to delineate the emerging profession. But PR, in turn, helped to delineate them: it established conventions for both business practice and media practice that continue to this day. As the term suggests, PR is about relationships. The business / media / PR triangle has been a cosy, but tangled, affair ever since the late nineteenth century, when the "captains of industry" began to put forward a new business ideology.

By the end of the nineteenth century the industrial revolution had generated large corporate capital wielded by a very few industrialists intent on consolidating their power. John D. Rockefeller Sr. and J. Pierpont Morgan were at the top of the list of the new millionaire magnates commanding vast empires in oil, steel, and banking, while conducting their own PR on a personal basis. The friends of important politicians, Rockefeller and Morgan could readily command the attention of presidents and Congress alike for the purpose of conveying their corporate desires. Similarly, in Canada at least as far back as 1879, much of the same executive personnel ran the Hudson's Bay Company, the Grand Trunk Railway, the Bank of Montreal, and the Canadian government. Just before the turn of the century these captains of industry put forward a new idea. As Alan Raucher writes in *Public Relations and Business from 1900 to 1929*: "In place of unrestricted competition of the laissez-faire model, combination was extolled. Giant corporations were, according to the new ideology, economically more efficient and socially beneficial."[9]

Behind this thinking was the desire to avoid the "instability" of market forces by creating huge horizontally-integrated trade associations and vertically-integrated businesses. J. Pierpont Morgan, the banker, had his fingers in so many industrial pies that the process of combining many companies into one giant corporation came to be known as "Morganizing industry". In 1901, for example, Morgan, using the power of his financial interests, succeeded in unifying all the components of the steel industry. Mining, smelting, refining, and manufacturing were all integrated into one big company, U.S. Steel. Recognizing that nickel production was vitally important to all aspects of the industry, especially weapons production, Morgan quickly bought up the mining rights to the Sudbury Basin in Canada, one of the two largest nickel-producing regions in the world. The result was the International Nickel Company, later known as Inco, incorporated in 1902 in New Jersey.[10]

J.P. Morgan's efforts in Canada coincided with the search by other companies for raw materials. In 1903 the United Fruit Company acquired 170,000 acres in Guatemala on which to grow bananas for export as a cash crop. William Van Horne, famous for his role in building the Canadian Pacific Railroad, helped put this deal together. In exchange for building a sixty-mile stretch of railway, the United Fruit Company (now known as United Brands) got its first foothold in Guatemala.[11]

At the same time, Canadian captains of industry like R.B. Bennett and W.M. (Max) Aitken (later Lord Beaverbrook) were also involved in company consolidations or "combines". Bennett acted as Aitken's agent in merging grain elevators and hydroelectric stations in the West. Together they controlled the Alberta Pacific Grain Company, which operated over four hundred grain elevators. Bennett was also part of the syndicate that formed the Canada Cement Company – a merger of thirteen companies that created a virtual monopoly.

These industrial tycoons often hired secret press agents to pass favourable information on to newspapers, trying to ensure favourable editorial comment and press coverage with regard to the growing concentration of power in business. These so-called "whitewashers" were also skilled at writing articles, under the bylines of their corporate employers, extolling the virtues of "economies of scale" and "monopoly rationalization" of business. These articles would then appear in major magazines and newspapers, helping to influence public opinion in favour of the expanding multinationals. While their employers engaged in their own personal lobbying behind closed doors, the corporate whitewashers were secretly planting stories to be picked up by the press. On the other hand, any unfavourable news or information was supposed to be ignored. The corporate policy of the time was to erect a barrier of strict silence in the face of any bad press.

Ivy Lee's PR strategies were thus a stunning reversal of previous conventions. Rather than deal in secret with the press, he found ways to openly court it – turning a train accident, for example, into a media event. Rather than write a magazine or news article to be "planted" in the press, he established ways to ensure favourable coverage from the press itself, through the press tour, the press conference, the pre-arranged interview, and, of course, the press release. Indeed, Lee realized that one modern strategy for corporate entities in trying times should be to deluge the press with information. It was a strategy that did not go unnoticed by the U.S. government, which had embarked on a war of world-wide proportions.

□

One of the young men hired by the government for the immense publicity effort surrounding World War I was Edward L. Bernays, nephew of Sigmund Freud. Now considered one of the founders of the PR profession, Bernays worked in Europe during the war, helping to put out a steady stream of morale-boosting pictures and cards, anti-propaganda propaganda, and information from the front lines. Back in the United States, the Committee on Public Information put out over 6,000 press releases, engaged 75,000 so-called "four-minute men" who gave patriotic speeches in local movie theatres and other public places, and got the Boy Scouts to deliver copies of Woodrow Wilson's speeches door to door. As Bernays later observed, "The wartime experience was a very revealing one in what communications can do. When I got back from Europe, I recognized that what we had done in wartime could be harnessed to peacetime pursuits."[12]

So it was World War I that revealed the scale on which PR could be practised, as well as the great potential that existed for the new industry. In his book *Crystallizing Public Opinion*, written in 1923, Bernays was a bit more forthright about what those "peacetime pursuits" might be: "It was the astounding success of propaganda during the War which opened the eyes of the intelligent few in all departments of life to the possibilities of regimenting the public mind."[13] Bernays's contribution to the emerging profession was to recognize that corporate and governmental "communications" had to be tailored not only for print but also for radio, the newsreel, the newspaper photographer, the wire-photo – any and all of the emerging mass media. Indeed, he recognized that the way to "regiment the public mind" was to court the media by providing "reportable events" specifically suited to each and every medium.

Just as the press release lays out the news story in a way that can be immediately transferred to the printed newspaper page, so Bernays recognized that the press conference, the press tour, the photo opportunity, and the pre-arranged interview should each be staged with the various media in mind. As he wrote: "The counsel on public relations not only knows what news value is, but knowing it, he is in a position to make news happen. He is the creator of events."[14] Bernays was especially interested in photographic images, more than words, and was skilled at thinking up news "gimmicks" for his clients: planned events with the visual potential to attract newsreel cameras and newspaper photographers.

The press release, the press conference, the photo opportunity, the pre-arranged interview, and the press tour have all, over the years, become fully integrated into the fabric of what we perceive as "the news". In other words, these techniques for courting the media have become so commonplace that we tend not to think of them as public-relations efforts at all. Yet it is possible to see each one as a way of pre-packaging "the news" for the media, of pointing the media in the desired direction. That certainly is how PR professionals themselves look at each of these tactics: as a way of "planting" news coverage suitable for their corporate or governmental clients. "Media people are busy too," says Stan Houston, president of one of Canada's biggest PR companies, The Houston Group. "They've got a job to do."

> And most of the people in public relations understand this. As a matter of fact, the great majority of them come from media and that's why they do understand it. They know better than to try to plant something that isn't worthwhile. The word "plant" has, I think, a bit of a stigma to it. I think we do try to engineer stories on behalf of our clients, but only if we think they're worthwhile, because we can project ourselves into the media's mind and realize what we would have said if somebody comes to us with that story. And that's the key.[15]

The Reagan administration proved itself to be unparalleled in its ability to project into the media's mind, and its gaggle of media advisors and PR pros was certainly not above using the "gimmick" or the red-herring trick to throw the press off the trail of a more important story. For instance, at the same time that Reagan announced his controversial "Star Wars" defence budget and the decision to allow the CIA to engage, for the first time, in domestic operations, the White House released the "news" that there was a Libyan hit squad out to assassinate top U.S. officials. The Libyan hit team was variously reported to have slipped into the United States from Canada, or to be hiding out in Mexico, or to have flown to Paris en route to Boston. It was high drama at the White House. Security was tightened. Presidential appearances were curtailed. The Canadian and Mexican borders were watched. Sketches of potential assassins were distributed to the press. But nothing happened. Several months went by and still nothing happened. Finally, the media began to question whether a Libyan hit squad ever existed.

In retrospect, not only was this "news" a diversion tactic focusing attention (of both press and public) away from other issues; it was also subtle PR preparation for Reagan's later bombing of Tripoli. Controlling the political agenda by controlling the media reached its apex in the 1980s. As Mark Hertsgaard writes, on the basis of interviews with former deputy White House press secretary Leslie Janka and former deputy chief of staff Michael Deaver:

> The Reagan White House "came to the conclusion that the media will take what we feed them," explained Janka. "They've got to write their own story every day. You give them their story, they'll go away. The phrase is 'manipulation by inundation'. You give them the line of the day, you give them press briefings, you give them facts, access to people who will speak on the record.... And you do that long enough, they're going to stop bringing their own stories, stop being investigative reporters of any kind, even modestly so." "I think that's true," added Deaver. "The only day I worried about was Friday, because it's a slow news day. That was the day that bothered me most, because if you didn't have anything, they'd go *find* something."[16]

In Canada the Mulroney government had utilized the federal deficit as a useful "news management" strategy, pointing the press away from any number of other things to focus on. As Linda McQuaig reveals, the government established "a massive public relations campaign identifying the deficit as a cancer threatening Canada's future".

In speech after speech, Mulroney and Wilson began trumpeting the evils of the deficit. The press picked up enthusiastically on the new theme of "belt-tightening" coming out of Ottawa. Commentators and editorial writers seemed to agree that Canadians were living beyond their means. The party was over, it was frequently said. Articles about the deficit sprang out of nowhere, full of huge multi-billion dollar numbers. Commentators started asking if the government had the "courage" and "political will" to do something about the situation.[17]

While PR expertise in media relations has reached an extraordinary degree of sophistication over the years, the mainstream media practitioners themselves – reporters, editors, producers – tend not to perceive the tactics for courting the press as anything but "neutral". Most would probably agree with Cameron Smith, former managing editor of *The Globe and Mail*, when he states:

> The mere calling of a press conference is almost a neutral act. What it does is allow the person, such as the Prime Minister or whoever, to be available for questions. If he says something worthwhile, it will get reported, and if he doesn't, it won't. What it does is give the reporters the opportunity to ask questions directly of him, so that in a sense it's not managing or arranging the news.[18]

But in its agenda-setting the press conference is no more neutral than language. One need only think of Reagan's constant press-conference references to the Contras as "freedom fighters", or the usual references to "terrorists" to summarize political complexities in other lands. Moreover, when the Prime Minister calls a press conference, what he says will get reported whether it is "worthwhile" or not.

One way of understanding these press "conventions" as PR news strategies is to compare them with the one thing that corporate and governmental PR would like to prevent: investigative reporting. From Ivy Lee right on up to this last gasp of the twentieth century, the PR goal has been to initiate the news story, to provide a "reportable event", so that (in the words of Michael Deaver) reporters won't go out and "*find* something". Another way to look at the press conference, the press release, the press tour, the photo opportunity, is that they are each strategies whereby media personnel are intended to be reactive, rather than active; responsive to the courtship dance rather than looking elsewhere, or (god forbid) digging out a different agenda for what will be news.

In 1961 a similar view was formulating in the mind of cultural historian Daniel J. Boorstin, who considered any event planned in advance "for the purpose of being reported" a "pseudo-event".[19] Connecting pseudo-events to the rise of the public-relations profession, Boorstin looked back on the previous fifty years and concluded: "In the last half century a larger and larger proportion of our experience, of what we read and see and hear, has come to consist of pseudo-events. We expect more of them and we are given more of them. They flood our consciousness."[20] The timing of Boorstin's thinking was, in retrospect, synchronistic – coinciding with the beginning of a decade in which an entire generation, just as media-hip as the PR professionals in many ways, began to dig relentlessly behind the facade of the entire military-industrial complex.

The rise of investigative reporting during the 1960s and early 1970s was just one aspect of the great PR crisis underway at the time. In terms of that deeper agenda of public-relations effort – what is called "the manufacture of consent" – a growing rejection was gathering in the populace that threatened virtually every aspect of Establishment business-as-usual. While not averse to planning their own pseudo-events, the 1960s generation was (for whatever reasons) highly skilled at seeing through "the golden age of bullshit", to use Fred C. Dobbs's down-home phrase.[21] The fact that that age has hit platinum has much to do with the specific PR strategies adopted to meet the crisis in corporate boardrooms and governmental offices from the sixties onwards.

The first step was to put the screws to investigative journalism at large. In Canada in 1966 the Pearson government killed "This Hour Has Seven Days", the CBC-TV show whose innovative reporting style was a threat to both the conventions of "objective" journalism and the corporate and governmental personas. Says former "Seven Days" production assistant Carol McIntyre, "Government spokesmen were used to being treated with kid gloves. Our show was getting too close to the bone."[22] The following year, 1967, CBC-TV broadcast Larry Gosnell's "Air of Death", a documentary on air pollution in Canada. It resulted in the calling of a Royal Commission, not to further investigate the causes of air pollution but to determine whether the TV program showed "bias". With regard to media relations, "uppity" journalists were being put in their place.

The second step on the public-relations front was to bite the bullet and admit (in private, of course) that on television, corporate and governmental spokespersons had a recurring tendency to look shifty-eyed, defensive, downright Nixonesque in their dealings with reporters. During the 1970s a whole rash of media training seminars, media advisory counsellors, and remedial media crisis experts sprang up to provide assistance to spokespeople under pressure. New companies like Communications Counselling of Canada (CCC), run by ex-CBS reporter Steve Rowan out of his Toronto office, offered media-grooming to PR spokesmen, corporate executives, and politicians:

> The basic training program is a series of three-day seminars, lots of interaction between the teacher and the participant. At the very basic level, Level One, it is handling straight questions, handling vague questions, handling emotionally-worded questions, making speeches, designing speeches, making speeches and then answering questions. Then it would go into areas of confrontation like radio or TV talk shows, call-in shows, and ultimately into training people to handle news interviews, radio, TV and newspaper, from the most friendly and supporting interviewer to the very high-level confronting type of interviewer like a Jack Webster in Vancouver or a Patrick Watson in Ottawa or a Fraser Kelly here in Toronto. It depends on how much training people want to get. We train them all the way from the basics up to the high-level / high-risk situations.[23]

To show his clients how to do it right, Rowan played news video-clips of leftist activists in action. "We admire some of the spokespersons for activist groups. They train us," he told me in 1981. As well, Rowan would invite in reporters or ex-reporters to go through the training exercises with his clients, doing before-and-after interviews to determine the scale of image-projection improvement. As a media training counsellor, Rowan did a brisk business until 1989 when his company ceased to be available through the Toronto directory. Perhaps by then everybody who needed media-grooming had gotten it.

But learning to speak in twenty-second "sound bites" and putting out a short, simple statement with a positive theme (without sweating or looking shifty-eyed) was not the full answer to the Establishment's PR crisis. Another step was to go beyond courting media practitioners and simply hire them. As Stan Houston recalls:

Perhaps the most spectacular case of this was in the early days of the oil crisis [1972] when the major oil companies first decided that they needed more public-relations help. People out of major news media – TV personalities who knew the medium, newspaper personalities who knew the medium – were recruited by the large oil companies to help them understand the whole medium of the message, if you want to put it that way.[24]

Of course, there were still some "bleeding hearts" and "nattering nabobs of negativism" rampant in the press and daring to stick their rude noses-for-news into what had always been sacrosanct territory, especially all those other areas of corporate PR: labour relations, financial relations, international relations, and (most important) public affairs PR.

This least-known branch of public relations (sometimes known as governmental relations) was becoming increasingly significant in the early 1970s, especially given the rise of citizens' activist groups, environmental groups, and others pressuring for more stringent regulation of the corporate sector and more fair legislation to meet the needs of ordinary citizens. Public-affairs specialist Larry Newman provides a useful summary of this branch of corporate PR:

> Wherever the operations of a corporation are impacted by public policy, that is public affairs. Now what does it mean practically? There's a whole field called "issues management", which is the attempt to forecast issues which will arise and how they will impact a company. There are specific issues-campaigns when you're working to get legislation passed, or stopped, or to influence regulation and the interpretation of regulation.[25]

John Sawatsky's book *The Insiders* gives a vivid portrait of some of the top Canadian public-affairs specialists who emerged in the late 1970s and throughout the 1980s to give counsel in this area to corporate clients.[26] As well, Linda McQuaig's *Behind Closed Doors* reveals the results of various financial and public-affairs PR activities on budget decisions.[27] In the United States, public-relations "issues management" has a somewhat longer history. Certainly the challenges of the 1960s led to increased efforts in this vein, coupled with the rise of the pollsters in the 1970s to forecast issues that would need "management".

Nevertheless, despite the fact that just about everything behind closed doors was stacked in their favour, the "corporate welfare bums" (David Lewis's term) recognized in the early 1970s that they were still losing the battle for public opinion, getting really poor ratings in the polls on their "credibility" and "honesty", while the popular heroes were people like the Greenpeace activists, or Ralph Nader, or (even more horrifying) Woodward and Bernstein at *The Washington Post*.

It was time for the double-whammy: (1) a fresh round of press-bashing, this time led by the corporate sector; and (2) bypassing the press entirely by buying space in the media for the Great Corporate Speak-Out.

□

Mobil Oil's head of PR, Herb Schmertz, is usually given the credit for leading the fray. In the early 1970s, during the energy crisis, Schmertz began kvetching in magazine and newspaper advocacy ads about how inadequate energy reporting was and how the oil industry was being depicted unfairly. Mobil's new "outspokenness" coincided with a decision at *The New York Times* to sell ad space on its op-ed page. Mobil immediately signed up, determined to "influence the influentials". As Randall Poe wrote in 1980: "Since 1972, in fact, the company has become almost a regular *Times* columnist, speaking out nearly as often as William Safire, Anthony Lewis, and Tom Wicker."[28]

By 1980 Mobil's advocacy ads were appearing in a wide variety of U.S. magazines and newspapers, and addressing a wide variety of topics. But Schmertz's favourite theme, the inadequacy of the press, was still paramount:

> The best test of truth is the power of the thought to get itself accepted in the competition of the market. But that means the thought has to make it into the market in the first place. And whether it gets that far often depends on the press.... Take energy reporting, for example. Some of it is superb. But, as an oil company, we are occasionally astonished and dismayed to see or read a quick, shallow treatment in the news concerning energy matters of profound domestic or international significance. This country can't make good decisions about business and energy unless the facts and the informed ideas on such matters have been explored by thorough and knowledgeable reporting....[29]

When U.S. TV networks refused to broadcast his advocacy ads, Schmertz retaliated with blasts at broadcast journalism, as this 1981 advocacy ad shows:

> The most powerful communications medium yet devised – television – will let you sell dog food and blue jeans, but never an idea dealing with a controversial subject of public importance. Not even an argument about such an idea. Not even facts if they are remotely connected with such an idea. To the television networks, controversial issues are objects of taboo that may be approached only by a special tribe: their own broadcast journalists.[30]

Gene Mater, vice-president of CBS Broadcast Group, put it somewhat differently, saying that to accept corporate advocacy ads would "allow a few voices – the voices of the affluent – to set the agenda for national debate and to exert a wholly disproportionate influence on the discussion of public issues in the broadcast media."[31] Schmertz called this policy "repressive censorship" and further mobilized his PR budget ($25 million in 1981) for the ongoing attack.

Meanwhile, other corporations quickly caught on to the new mood. Kaiser Aluminum and Chemical Corporation, fuming because of an investigative piece done by ABC-TV on its marketing of hazardous products, placed a major advocacy ad campaign across the national print media, which read:

> The American system of justice is founded on a simple principle: the accused has a right to be fairly heard in his own defense, and to confront and cross examine his accuser. This principle, more than any other, defines the difference between freedom and tyranny. Yet today, here in America, charges are aired before tens of millions of people without fair opportunity for the accused to respond. They call it "investigative television journalism". We call it "trial by television".[32]

Similarly, United Technologies – weapons-maker par excellence – launched its series of advocacy ads, including one under the banner heading "Where the Media Elite Stand" that stated: "Some 54 percent of leading journalists count themselves as liberals. Only 19 percent describe themselves as right of center." The "liberal" journalists, the ad said, "show special fondness for welfare capitalism. Some 68 percent believe the government should substantially reduce the income gap between rich and poor." United Technologies also complained that this media elite believed that "U.S. economic exploitation has contributed to poverty in the Third World."[33]

By 1980 U.S. corporate PR departments were spending an estimated $1 billion per year on such advocacy advertising,[34] much of it devoted to press-bashing, but all of it devoted to bypassing reporters by buying newspaper and magazine space to present the corporate point of view. Shortly thereafter an extensive survey of independent TV stations and network-affiliated stations revealed that most were prepared to accept corporate advocacy ads despite the stance of their newtwork's flagship stations.[35]

In addition, U.S. corporations began to produce their own "news" segments to be distributed to local and independent TV stations for broadcast during the nightly news-hour. Using all the codes of news broadcasting – including a reporter-type interviewing the spokesperson of the company, cutaway shots to the relevant scene, and "backgrounder" footage – these pseudo-news giveaways were distributed especially to cable companies and budget-starved local news outfits willing to broadcast the segments as part of their news-hour.[36] Utilities advocating nuclear power became one of the primary users of this form of public "education" in the United States. It is now apparently considered standard for companies to distribute videotapes to local stations as "free programming". As Schmertz put it early in the game, "Corporations are not in business to manipulate public opinion, but if their livelihood is threatened – or if they perceive a threat to the national welfare in some proposed government action – they should speak out."[37]

The Reagan government in 1980 was readily revealing its hostility towards the press. William C. McDonald, Reagan's executive director of the Federal Energy Regulatory Commission, cautioned his new federal agency chiefs: "Never forget that an adversary relationship will always exist between you and the Washington press, which today consists of hundreds of graduates of the Woodward and Bernstein School of Journalism. So think defensively. Hire a first-rate PR man in whom you have 100 percent confidence, and follow his advice. Never meet with reporters unless your press secretary is present."[38]

It didn't take long for the trend to catch on in Canada. *The Globe and Mail* started courting the advocacy advertising dollar in 1980, with a campaign slogan that must have been somewhat demoralizing for its reporters: "If you want it said right, say it yourself". The smaller copy continued:

It's remarkable how often people react in righteous indignation when a newspaper story does not reflect their own point of view. Fortunately the freedom of the press allows for a response through the time-honored tradition of letters to the editor. But there's another aspect of freedom of the press that for too long was ignored. That's freedom to advocate a point of view through the use of corporate advertising.[39]

If corporations wanted to reach "the kinds of people who can influence change", the *Globe* argued, the best way to do this was through its own pages. Within a little more than a year, Canadian media critic Morris Wolfe was estimating that "as much as 20 per cent of the *Globe*'s advertising now consists of advocacy ads of one form or another. It seems to me that what we've done through advocacy advertising is allow people who have money more freedom of speech than people who don't have money."[40]

Catching the wave from the United States, Canada's The Haughton Group put out its big print ad: "A question for the people attacking free enterprise: Are you against freedom, enterprise, or both?"[41] Imperial Oil launched its advocacy campaign in 1981: "Allegations of a consumer rip-off by oil companies are going to be examined in a public inquiry. Our response? The sooner the better!"[42] The Bank of Montreal jumped in too, joining the fight to tell the corporate side of the story:

Recent bank earnings have prompted some criticism of Canada's chartered banks. The charges hold first that the banks are exploiting the country's unprecedentedly high interest rates, and second, that bank earnings are "excessive". On both counts, we believe the facts present a different picture.[43]

Imperial Oil came back with another salvo: "Imperial Oil is creating jobs by investing $1 billion in Canada this year [1981]. Profits make this possible.... When you hear about oil company profits, we hope you will remember oil company investments and how they help create employment."[44] Then the Bank of Nova Scotia joined the fray: "For the last little while, we at the Bank of Nova Scotia have been publishing messages of optimism in hopes of providing a counterbalance to the messages of doom and gloom, and to the pundits' cries of wolf, and to all those who feel that the sky is falling on the Canadian economy."[45]

While Canadian corporations were putting out the corporate hard-line message in the midst of the recession, they were also, in 1981, collectively spending $122 million in public-affairs lobbying behind closed doors – a figure that does not include expenditures on lobbying by individual corporations.[46]

The corporate advocacy of the early 1980s was generally a retread of Agnew's charge of "nattering nabobs of negativism" in the press. *Saturday Night* magazine took a similar tack in trying to attract more advocacy ad dollars: "If the world is going to hell in a handcart, it's a better-made handcart than last year's.... We can't help you reach the prophets of doom. But we could help you reap the profits of success. What are your plans for Saturday Night?"[47]

The Canadian government also jumped on the PR bandwagon, becoming the top advertiser in the country by 1979 in annual expenditures, and spending $60 million on "information" in 1980. By 1981 the figure was approaching $100 million and still climbing. Supply and Services Minister Jean-Jacques Blais let slip the subtext behind all the expensive rhetoric. "Government is too complex nowadays to rely on 'policy by press release'," he declared. "Programs must be explained – and not by reporters."[48] The hasty little qualifying phrase at the end speaks volumes.

The issue, of course, was language: the naming and clarification of events. For example, Litton Industries, makers of the guidance systems for the Cruise missile, placed a newspaper ad after the bombing of its plant: "To a lot of wonderful people: thank you." The ad singled out those (presumably few) "members of the media who understood and correctly reported that our company is not a missile manufacturer but an electronics company". While the tone of these Canadian advocacy ads was less strident than their U.S. counterparts, the message was clear: the "liberal" press was not to be trusted.

The full irony of the situation, however, was revealed by the mainstream media's response to the brickbats. Rather than hold firm to at least the principle of an adversarial role, given the conditions of our society in which power is concentrated in the hands of a few, the press began to cave in like a collapsed lung. CBS-TV's "Sixty Minutes" broadcast an entire hour (September 7, 1981) in which a panel of critics, including Mobil's Herb Schmertz, was able to air grievances about the program's reporting tactics. The show was on the defensive – precisely what the corporate critics had wanted. Nevertheless, Schmertz was still not entirely satisfied.

"They only dealt with one issue," he complained after the show, "the ambush-confrontational interview. There are many other issues relating to 'Sixty Minutes' that they didn't deal with, but I knew going into the show that would be the case."[49] Schmertz wanted the show to also cover "the whole system of editing, the whole system of advocacy, the whole system of sources, the whole system of the timing of their shows to tie-in with Congressional hearings to skew the debate in a particular way". All this was part of what Schmertz at the time was calling "accusatory journalism". When I suggested that what he was doing was dangerous, it set him off. "Why is anybody speaking out on any issue dangerous?" he growled. "I would say that somebody who thinks that's 'dangerous' really has no faith in the First Amendment or the intelligence of the American public to decide important issues." What was particularly galling to Schmertz was that he had seen instances where the TV networks had violated their own policy. "I have seen ads supporting and advocating 55 mile-an-hour speed limits," he told me. "I've seen ads urging energy conservation. The other side of energy conservation, for example, would be ads urging increased energy development in the U.S. Those ads they won't take."

After the "Sixty Minutes" cave-in, ABC-TV then launched a program called "Viewpoint" to regularly give a forum to critics of the network's news coverage. The first show featured Kaiser Aluminum and Chemical Corporation rebutting the investigative piece done on its hazardous products by ABC's "20 / 20". Then *Time* magazine issued a ten-page cover story called "Accusing the Press: What Are Its Sins?" in which we learned that "the suspicious attitude among reporters leads to negativism in news coverage" and that "critics also fault the capital's press corps for preoccupation with politics." In Canada a rash of new business publications and TV shows like "Venture" helped to satisfy corporate desires for "positive" reporting.

□

Not surprisingly, an opinion poll in 1983 showed that the public's "confidence" in the press had reached a ten-year low: only 13.7 per cent of the population were "confident" about the abilities of the press. The corporate press-bashing had obviously paid off. But the next move probably surprised even Herb Schmertz.

Reagan, the Great Communicator, ordered a military invasion of Grenada and a complete press blackout surrounding the affair. For Leslie Janka, a deputy White House press secretary who resigned over the Grenada events, the whole Reagan administration was pure PR: "This was a PR outfit that became president and took over the country." The administration may have also had to take care of the standard government necessities — "make a budget, run foreign policy" — but for Janka, "their first, last, and overarching activity was public relations".[50] Two of Reagan's impressive team of PR pros — Mike Deaver (deputy chief of staff) and Craig L. Fuller (director of cabinet administration) — had previously worked for the Hannaford Company, the PR firm hired by Guatemala to improve its image. Since "killing off the news" had worked for the Guatemalan regime, they must have felt it was also worth a try for the Grenada invasion.

And indeed, their PR gamble paid off. ABC-TV stated that 99 per cent of the mail from viewers supported Reagan's press blackout. NBC-TV's viewers, in over five hundred letters and calls, favoured banning the press by a ratio of five to one. *Time* magazine's mail ran eight to one against the press. A survey of U.S. daily newspapers found that letters to the editor were running three to one in favour of Reagan's exclusion of the press.[51]

Mark Hertsgaard, author of *On Bended Knee: The Press and the Reagan Presidency*, writes:

> On a daily basis, the Reagan men applied a two-pronged news management strategy: Control your message by keeping reporters away from a scripted president, and capture television's attention with choreographed, visually attractive photo opportunities that reinforce the chosen "line of the day". The line of the day (a concept once associated with totalitarian, not democratic, governments) was, in turn, derived from extensive public opinion polling, polling aimed less at learning what citizens truly desired from their government than at discovering what catch phrases and gimmicks would appeal to their fears and prejudices.[52]

For Hertsgaard, "The objective was not simply to tame the press but to transform it into an unwitting mouthpiece of the government."

It probably shouldn't surprise us that the major U.S. media story of the 1980s, Iranscam, was actually first unearthed by a small political magazine reporting on the Middle East. Nor should it surprise us that a major figure in that whole dirty deal now sits in the Oval Office. Since media relations has not co-opted much of the power of the press, with government and corporate media advisors highly skilled in creating "reportable events", photo-ops, and the necessary "line of the day", the great masked ball continues.

In Canada the Mulroney government, taking many of its cues from Reagan's media strategy, has acquired its own coating of Teflon over the years, assisted in part by the fact that by 1984 the federal government had become accustomed to spending at least $266 million per year on "information" disseminating policy and point of view.[53] Of particular concern, of course, has been the variety of tax "reforms" and budgetary changes brought in by the Tories. Linda McQuaig informs us of a standard media-relations procedure that might now be well-known, the "media lock-up":

These media lock-ups, which are customary before government budgets as well, are clearly designed to influence the media's reaction to government proposals. Journalists are allowed an advance preview of the tax changes in the lock-up, so that they can have their reports largely prepared by the time the government documents are officially released to the public. But the circumstances of this advance viewing are strictly controlled. Once they enter, journalists are not allowed to communicate in any way with the outside world. Pay telephones are stripped of their outside connections. Guards patrol every exit with walkie-talkies. Inside, the journalists are provided with endless coffee and food ... and are surrounded by swarms of Finance Department officials, who readily explain and interpret the tax changes. Whatever the question – corporate tax, personal tax, sales tax, fiscal outlook, economic impact, fairness – there is a willing expert there, ready to sit down and provide private tutoring for the bewildered journalist. An aspiring cult leader could probably pick up a few useful ideas on mind-control methods from observing one of these lock-ups.[54]

For corporations, a favourite strategy in the whole post-1960s "legitimacy gap" PR crisis was to simply buy up the media. The 1970s and 1980s saw the most astounding media buy-outs of the century, usually by highly diversified conglomerates looking to expand

into infotainment, information, and news. The extraordinary con-
solidation in media ownership continued with even greater frenzy as
the 1980s drew to a close, with the merger of Warner Brothers and
Time Inc. (now called Time Warner Inc.); Rupert Murdoch's $3 bil-
lion purchase of Walter Annenberg's Triangle Publications; the decision of Gulf & Western (now called Paramount Communications
Inc.) to concentrate on planetary media ownership; and Maclean
Hunter's takeover of Selkirk Communications Ltd. This rapid concentration in media ownership was aided by conservative governments who embraced the principles of deregulation and privatization, including major funding cuts to public broadcasting throughout Europe, Britain, Canada, and the United States. As the buying
spree continues unabated, media analysts are predicting that by the
early 1990s fewer than ten corporate conglomerates will own and
control most of the world's major newspapers, magazines, broadcasting stations, book publishers, movie studios, and record and
videocassette industries.

And when all else fails, there is always the libel suit to be slapped
on the investigative reporter and her or his media outlet – a potent
weapon for maintaining self-censorship on the part of the press. Currently, journalists hesitate to invoke the name "Reichmann" for fear
of bringing down some form of hideous repercussion.

During the 1980s all these tactics for handling the legitimacy gap
have come together with the result that, judging by mainstream
media content, the new "heroes" of these neoconservative times are
the millionaires and yuppie business people who figure prominently
in the glowing coverage devoted to their "success". In a country in
which one out of every six Canadians lives below the poverty level,
that focus is reprehensible.

In spring 1989 a new angle was added to government media relations. A Canadian journalist, Doug Small (Ottawa bureau chief for
Global-TV News), was charged by the RCMP with possession of a
stolen document in the events surrounding the Wilson budget leaks.

But finance minister Michael Wilson himself was quite safe.
Whenever rumours surfaced about his possible resignation over the
matter, the financial pages quickly filled with threatening headlines
about the Canadian dollar "buckling" and Bay Street's unease. Similarly, the budget itself was strongly buttressed by a variety of PR
tactics.

In advance of its release, Wilson hired a task force including communications consultant and trouble-shooter Nancy Jamieson and issues-management specialist Heather Conway, a consultant from Ottawa's largest PR firm, Public Affairs International (PAI), to predict the fallout from the forthcoming budget bombshell and advise ways of selling it to a reluctant public.[55] A three-pronged PR strategy was developed, including a $2.7 million advertising blitz in TV, radio, and newspapers to convince us that increased taxes and slashed federal programs were a winning solution for that suddenly hideous spectre, the national debt. One radio ad intoned: "The money Ottawa spends on health services, welfare, family allowances, pensions and income supplements combined – that's just about what we'll spend this year on interest on the national debt. Year after year, government after government, we've borrowed against the future and now we can see the cost." Neglecting to include the amount Ottawa spends on PR, this multi-media blitz was to be followed by high-profile speeches from Michael Wilson and interviews with selected journalists (prong two), then a series of endorsements for the budget from respected non-Tories (prong three). A senior Conservative strategist remarked, "We're trying to promote third party endorsements because it worked so well for us on the [free] trade issue."[56]

But even Edward Bernays, in his wildest dreams about "regimenting the public mind", could not have foreseen a series of technological developments that would make his goal not only ridiculously easy, but also the standard procedure of the times. Behind those two "communications" strategies that typify the post-1960s PR milieu – changing our expectations about what is possible, and changing the symbolism for corporate and governmental performance – is the pollster, the leading figure in the whole public-relations profession. As media analyst Jean Baudrillard has observed, "It is no longer necessary that anyone *produce* an opinion, all that is necessary is that all *reproduce* public opinion."[57]

4

The Power of the Pollsters

When a television director once suggested to Harry Truman that his tie was inappropriate for TV, Truman stared pityingly with those blue eyes for about ten seconds. "Does it really matter?" he asked. "Because if while I'm talking about Korea, people are asking each other about my necktie, it seems to me we're in a great deal of trouble."

EDMUND CARPENTER

SOME FORTY YEARS after this exchange between Truman and an unknown TV director, things have changed. Now a "focus group" would be convened, well in advance of the telecast, to determine the appropriate colour symbolism and patterned motif, the shape and precise knot of the presidential tie to match the intended mood of the televised speech. Harry would have the benefit of an in-depth psychographic survey, indicating, perhaps, that 42 per cent of the upscale, influential populace consider this particular tie troublesome.

The contemporary media advisor would answer that of course such things really do matter, that in the age of image-politics these details can make the difference in the perceived legitimacy and credibility of any political leader. Indeed, a complex apparatus of media expertise exists primarily to ensure that such tiny details do not sabotage the smooth unfolding of the political will. It is as though, during the past forty years of television's rise to socio-political hegemony, things like Truman's tie (was it polka-dotted? A bow-tie? A polka-dotted bow-tie?) have expanded to fill the entire screen of our collective imaginal brain-pans. And yes, we're in a great deal of trouble.

But the term "image-politics" can be misleading, especially because it tends to direct our focus to effects rather than causes; thus, the term makes us think of things like John Turner's speech-coach during the 1988 election, or George Bush's cowboy hat and hang-'em-high rhetoric to combat the wimp and sleaze factors plaguing him in the early days of his '88 campaign. The conventional understanding of the term "image-politics" was nicely summarized in autumn of that year by media consultant Patricia Adams: "Mulroney is so damn well packaged that you could turn him around and expect to see a list of ingredients on his back."[1]

But the real basis for image-politics is the coded images in *our* heads. As veteran U.S. political media advisor and adman Tony Schwartz puts it, "The goal of a media advisor is to tie up the voter and deliver him [sic] to the candidate. So it is really the voter who is packaged by the media, not the candidate."[2]

To understand the full implications of this tantalizing statement – which applies equally to both consumers and voters in contemporary life – we must delve into the dismaying complexities and hideous obfuscations of that key linchpin, that primary mediator between the public and the power-bloc, the pollster. If behind the media gatekeepers stands the public-relations profession skilled in media relations, then behind the PR profession stands the pollster. Over the past two decades, in-depth attitudinal polling (otherwise known as "psychographics") has become absolutely central to every aspect of public relations and business-as-usual, including political business-as-usual.

In the current era of the "sound bite", the photo-op, and "image doctors" for every corporate and governmental media event, attitudinal polling is the crucial first step in a sequence of activities designed to address the images in our heads. Not surprisingly, the layers of mystification surrounding the politics of polling are as thick as the leather of Allan Gregg's trademark jacket.

□

The telephone interviewers hang up their backpacks and athletic tote-bags, their umbrellas and Eaton's shopping bags, and gather in the posh sixth-floor meeting room of Summerhill Research – the polling branch of Allan Gregg's Decima Research Ltd., located in the Rosedale area of uptown Toronto. It is 5:00 p.m., the time when most people are finishing the daily grind, but for the fifty-or-so members of the Decima telephone staff – many of them high-school and university students – the working "day" is just beginning.

The supervisor hands out the evening's questionnaire. This time it's an attitudinal survey being conducted for the major chemical companies, who want to know how Canadians feel about their industry. A quick glance at the graffiti scrawls in any urban area would provide an answer, but the companies are interested in a far more detailed and in-depth psychological grasp of the public attitude. Not just the numbers pro and con, but the mind-set behind the opinion: the feelings, fears, beliefs, mental images, bits of information and knowledge, the media clichés, the prevailing attitudes, all of the things that generate the respondent's opinion. As the telephone interviewers are advised to say when a respondent claims to know little about the issue being surveyed, "In this survey it's not what you know that counts. Rather it's what you happen to think that is important. There are no right or wrong answers; we are just interested in learning about your experiences and how you feel about things."

The supervisor goes through the questionnaire section by section, pointing out the potential trouble-spots in the twenty-three-page survey, and she informs the telephone crew that the optimal time for completing this particular in-depth probe is thirty-seven minutes per respondent. Obviously, to get a good representative sample of more than a thousand completed surveys, the crew is going to be dealing with this particular questionnaire for a couple of nights running.

As the briefing finishes the interviewers pick up their sharpened pencils and stacks of questionnaires and retire to their individual cubicles, where a long list of phone numbers waits beside each phone. The numbers have been randomly selected by computer, but they accord with the base-line demographic sample frame chosen for this survey – urban middle class. Across Canada, the first round of fifty telephones start to ring. "Hello," says the Decima interviewer in each cubicle. "Today we're talking to people in your neighbourhood about issues facing us all."

Decima Research Ltd., chaired by Canadian polling *Wunderkind* Allan Gregg, is part of the massive and sophisticated polling apparatus that has been erected across North America since the early 1970s. Official pollster for the Progressive Conservative Party, and with an impressive battery of corporate clients, Decima is the leading company in Canada specializing in psychographics: meticulous profiles of consumer / voter attitudes matched with conventional demographic data (sex, age, race, income, education, occupation, location). "I try not to use the word 'psychographics'," Gregg tells me. "More simply, people have a shared psychology and shared beliefs."[3] Nevertheless, five nights a week, every week of the year, year-in and year-out, Decima (and similar companies across the continent) telephone thousands of people who are willing to bare their psyches to some telephoning stranger during a forty-minute probe.

The phenomenon itself would be worthy of analysis for what it may indicate about societal anomie and / or the telephone as terrorist weapon of modern-day marketing, but more important is the question of what happens to the resulting psychographic data. The answer is that it is the first step in a chain of media operations that are now entirely typical of our times.

An historical example from the early days of Decima's ten-year rise to success nicely indicates the sequential elements in the chain. In the summer of 1980 the Ottawa lobbyist for the Canadian Petroleum Association, Jamie Deacey, hired Decima to conduct a survey of the public's attitude towards the oil industry.[4] Gregg's resulting probe revealed that, by and large, Canadians perceived oil companies as rich, greedy, untrustworthy tax-dodgers who could not be counted on to supply Canada's energy needs. While these results may have been somewhat shocking for the corporate sponsor of the survey, the findings were crucial for taking remedial action.

The Association launched a national advocacy advertising campaign in newspapers, magazines, and television – fronted in the early years by former CBC-TV newsman Ken Colby. The ads extolled the virtues and achievements of the oil industry, and particularly addressed (for the purpose of remedying them) the weak points in the institutional image revealed by the attitudinal survey. Colby's familiar presence (his "recognition factor", to use the jargon) was useful for lending an aura of objectivity, and even news-value, to the ads.

Meanwhile Decima continued to poll for subtle shifts in public opinion during the initial ad campaign. This facilitated the fine-tuning of imagery and language used in subsequent ads so they would speak to the concerns and beliefs of the desired demographic constituency. Similarly, the psychographic data was useful for designing other aspects of the public-relations campaign, especially the "news management" side: press conferences, answers to report-ers' questions, press releases, speeches by corporate spokespeople, photo opportunities to generate favourable press coverage.

Coinciding with this campaign, many of the corporate spokespeo-ple had been getting some necessary media-grooming from trainers like Steve Rowan, who specialized in coaching corporate and govern-mental honchos in the midst of an image crisis. "Basically," Rowan coached them, "the key is to build answers based on a simple for-mula that starts out with a short, simple statement directly and hon-estly answering the question, and as soon as possible, launching a positive theme, since most questions that reporters tend to focus on are negatives. The second step," according to Rowan, "is to support every statement that you make in your short, simple statement and your positive theme with a fact, an example, an analogy, or a refer-ence: that is, to document what you're saying with specific evi-dence. And the third step is to either switch to the subject that you want to be talking about in this particular interview, or to lay out a benefit of what it is you're doing."[5] As John Sawatsky reports in *The Insiders*, the result of this lengthy but dedicated public-relations campaign (dutifully tracked by Decima for its client) was that "the oil industry's 'honest' rating rose from 32 to 54 per cent in three years".[6]

What must be emphasized about this now-typical chain of events is that attitudinal survey findings do not necessarily lead to any real changes in the sponsoring client's actual behaviour. Feedback from the public vis-à-vis the oil industry, for instance, did not noticeably generate any industry housecleaning in those problem areas uncovered by the survey. Indeed, as Linda McQuaig reports with regard to Shell Canada during all this PR activity:

In its 1982 statement, it reported income taxes of $152 million on profits of $302 million. This, the report calculated, gave the company an effective tax rate of 50.4 percent — a hefty rate by any standard. In fact, Shell deferred $199 million in taxes that year through writing off investments in plant and equipment at an artificially fast rate. This wiped out the company's $152 million tax bill, leaving Shell tax-free that year. In fact, Shell actually ended up with a credit of $47 million, which could be used to reduce taxes in future years. While this was clearly a much more pleasing picture to Shell's management and shareholders, this wasn't the story the company wanted to project to the public. By reporting a tax rate of 50.4 percent, Shell looked like it was making a sizeable contribution to Canadian society. Clearly Canadians would be much more inclined to regard Shell as a good corporate citizen if they believed the company contributed $152 million to the national treasury than if they realized that the treasury ended up owing Shell $47 million.[7]

Obviously, during those three intense years of oil industry PR activity the housecleaning was directed at the perceptions in the public mind, the images in our heads. Paraphrasing Tony Schwartz's dictum, we could say that it was the consumer-citizenry which got repackaged by the media campaign and delivered over to the corporate client.

Thus those two "communications strategies" referred to by Professor Prakesh Sethi for closing the legitimacy gap – changing our expectations about what is possible in terms of corporate behaviour, and changing the symbolism of that behaviour itself – depend upon first knowing as much as possible about *us*. The rise of psychographic polling during the past twenty years has generated a standard sequence of events for corporate and governmental public-relations activity, a sequence that is actually a loop both starting and ending with us: (1) conduct an in-depth attitudinal survey that identifies the image problems; (2) mount an advocacy ad campaign and other "news management" strategies based on the polling; (3) reflect back to the public the images and buzzwords, the rhetoric and symbols, that we want.

This whole process is, as Baudrillard notes, an "integrated circuit of question / answer", creating a "simulacrum of public opinion" which is "a mirror of opinion analogous in its way to that of the Gross National Product: imaginary mirror of the productive forces, without regard to their social ends or lack thereof".[8] This simulacrum becomes, then, the explanation (and indeed the justification) of decisions made outside the loop, outside that integrated circuit in which we, the public, are trapped by public opinion itself. As the McDonald's hymn says, "We do it all for you."

"Public opinion," writes Baudrillard, "is par excellence at the same time medium and message. And the polls that inform it are the incessant imposition of the medium as message. In this sense they are of the same nature as TV and the electronic media, which ... are also only a perpetual game of question / answer, an instrument of perpetual polling."[9]

There is, however, a potential break in that integrated circuit, revealed (ironically enough) by the telephone interviewers' response to the respondent: "In this survey, it's not what you know that counts. It's what you happen to think ... we are just interested in learning about your experiences and how you feel about things." The semantic nuance here between knowing and thinking reveals the key to stepping outside of the circularity. If we really *know* something, no amount of rhetoric or imagery can affect that; thus we are vulnerable to being repackaged only in those areas where our knowledge is uncertain, incomplete, nebulous, hazy. Similarly, if we understand the meaning of our own experiences (including our mediated "experiences") they cannot so easily be mirrored back to us in ways that are ultimately exploitive. But in a society in which much of importance happens behind closed doors, beyond our knowledge, we are meant to be vulnerable because of what we don't know.

For example, in 1985 Decima began conducting in-depth attitudinal polling on the issue of free trade with the United States. In 1985, it is fair to say, the amount of information available about the deal was still minimal. Nevertheless, Decima began to gather useful psychographics on a continuing basis. "By 1987," says my Decima deep-throat (I'll call her / him Silkwood), "we did a long survey on free trade – you know, a twenty-three-page questionnaire. We interviewed way over a thousand people on the phone, probing their hopes and fears, their opinions and beliefs about the free-trade deal. It was awful. I knew it was being done to help somebody write propaganda, whoever was sponsoring the survey. What people don't know is that these attitudinal polls are the basis for propaganda."

Psychographic polling is now so commonplace that, in Canada, it has even become a kind of weird and twisted form of pop-culture ritual. For the fifth year in a row, Canada's weekly newsmagazine again devoted virtually half of its first issue of the year to the *Maclean's* / Decima Poll – twenty-three published pages of numbers, charts, statistical data, and personal interviews gathered by some fifty *Maclean's* staff members and the polling expertise of Decima Research Ltd.

This massive annual cover-story – entitled "A Spotlight on Canadians" in the January 2, 1989 issue – takes up far more pages than *Maclean's* would devote to any news story during the rest of the year. Editor Kevin Doyle explains: "For one thing, it provides the most comprehensive post-election analysis of voters and voting patterns, based on 1,500 interviews, ever done in Canada. For another, it is one of the first attempts to measure changes in the attitudes of Canadians as the world rushes toward the end of one century and prepares to begin another – and a new millennium."[10]

But there's another angle from which to view this gargantuan *Maclean's* / Decima Poll, now done five years running. It is a component in the build-up of the necessary psychographic data base – national in scope and increasingly long-term – through which trends in the public psyche may be accurately pinpointed and targeted for the purpose of forecasting issues to be managed.

"*Maclean's* is one of our clients," says Gregg. "We do the poll for them. We say the data is ours and the information is theirs. But look. We already have a *huge* data base. We will merge Census data, we subscribe to InfoGlobe, we access all kinds of data. But the most important, for our purposes, is always up-to-the-minute data. The *Maclean's* poll provides historical context." In this sense, the annual survey is a spin-off of Gregg's tutelage under the most important pollster in the United States.

Hard to believe, but it was only a dozen years earlier that Allan Gregg was Allan Who? That was before Richard Wirthlin, pollster for Ronald Reagan since 1970, started a joint-venture company in Canada and uttered his prophetic remark: "Allan," he said, "we're going to make you the number-one pollster in this country. You watch."[11]

□

Back in the mid-1970s political polling in Canada was still in a primitive stage, focusing primarily on so-called "horse-race polls" (who's ahead?) and relying on U.S. pollsters and political advisors for campaign strategy. The Conservatives, for instance, had perennially hired Bob Teeter (pollster for Nixon, then Ford, then Bush) to oversee their campaigns. But the feeling within the party was that Teeter tended to simply recycle his last Republican campaign strategy when advising the Tories.

At the same time that the Conservatives were becoming disenchanted with Teeter, a young university student arrived to work in the research office of Tory headquarters. Allan Gregg impressed his superiors with his abilities and political savvy, and in the summer of 1978 Bill Neville, top PC strategist and advisor, nominated Gregg for an exchange program sponsored by the U.S. State Department.

Gregg applied for a ten-day consulting tour across the United States to interview and learn from the leading U.S. pollsters and political consultants. The State Department approved the idea and made arrangements for Gregg to meet the top guns in the field. On his whirlwind tour through Washington and Texas Gregg encountered the cream of the crop, but it was in California that he met *la crème de la crème* in a coterie of political advisors that included Peter Hart, Pat Caddell, Lance Torrance, Matt Reese, Stu Spencer, and Richard Wirthlin.

It was Wirthlin, however, who impressed Gregg the most. When it came to polling, nobody in the late-1970s Western world had a better grasp of the intricacies and techniques of the business. Certainly nobody else could even come close in those three primary keys of the polling science: simulations, targeting, and tracking. And, equally important, nobody had a more thoroughly detailed, psychologically convoluted, and demographically correlated national data base than Richard Wirthlin. By the time of Gregg's visit Wirthlin had cranked up his Santa Ana polling apparatus to a fever pitch, poised to launch his Main Man right on course to the Big Enchilada.

Roland Perry's study of the twenty-year Wirthlin-Reagan collaboration, *Hidden Power*, reminds us that polling is an offspring of military "wargaming", which found high-tech formats in the late 1950s via computer developments.[12] Military and political scientists at the Pentagon glommed onto the marvels of the technology for running complex simulations of battle – giving numerical weights to factors like population densities, opposing military strengths, precedents in battle, and specific environmental conditions – thereby creating scenarios that could be quickly analysed to yield probability outcomes. Wargaming by computer allowed detailed, moment-by-moment adjustments to changing factors in the Cold War political scene.

Big business immediately saw the usefulness of such techniques for developing marketing models and strategies. When the new line of more accessible hardware, like the IBM 360 series, came on the market in the mid-1960s, business was already primed to engage in its own forms of wargaming. For example, a company could run a wide range of production variables, demographic factors, market situations, and "what if?" scenarios to calculate probable outcomes. (What if we introduce a new brand of breakfast cereal into the market next year? Is the market saturated? Can it stand another competitor if we position our product for the adult market? What if our price per item is two cents lower than the nearest competitor? What if we pitch it to the female "pink collar" market? What if we launch in August?) The computer could handle such factors by correlating weighted numerical equivalents, and spew out a model outcome for each scenario.

Richard Wirthlin had helped develop such marketing simulation models for business during the experimental years, and he quickly recognized the potential usefulness of such strategies and marketing techniques for the political arena. In 1969 he started his own company, Decision Making Information (DMI), and began to build up the necessary demographic data base. Besides accessing every available statistical agency in the country, DMI hired a large crew of telephone interviewers for attitudinal survey work covering a wide range of consumer / voter issues, concerns, and beliefs.

By the time he joined Reagan's team of political advisors during the 1970 California gubernatorial race, Wirthlin was perfecting his "Political Information System" (PINS), a complex mass of psychographic data on specific target groups across the country. PINS is based on five key elements: up-to-the-minute attitudinal survey work, fixed demographic information, historical voting patterns for every county in the country, on-going assessment of political party strength in each state, and subjective analysis by Wirthlin's team.

"For twenty years," states Roland Perry, "Wirthlin has computer-filed his own polling data in the hundreds of campaigns he has run for Republicans, along with quantities of census figures, information from 37 federal departments, voting history figures from every county, and extensive market survey work for scores of American businesses." As a result, says Perry, "Wirthlin's computers can provide him in an instant with the political preferences and behavior of 110 categories of the American electorate."[13]

In 1970 this computer targeting was a pioneering strategy in political campaigning, used by Reagan's team to tailor ads and speeches and direct mail for specific audiences. By the time of Reagan's first presidential race, targeting had become so refined that it could pinpoint the prevailing psychographics of individual city neighbourhoods.

Another technique that Wirthlin borrowed from consumer marketing to apply to the 1970 campaign was tracking. It was this technique that most impressed Gregg during his 1978 visit. In the product world, once that new breakfast cereal is launched it must be closely followed to provide feedback on marketing strategies. (In which individual stores within the fifty major markets is it moving? Which TV time-slots are delivering the desired consumer groups? What effect is the special display in supermarket shelves having? How is our product-recognition factor? What do focus groups feel about the words "high in fibre" on the package?)

Wirthlin recognized that tracking would help a political candidate's team to know whether specific speeches, events, and "news management" techniques were having an impact on the public. This could be determined best by daily attitudinal polling in order to precisely graph the ongoing course of a campaign. In the United States, tracking has now become so standard that it is used continuously, while the pollster's client is in office, to monitor his or her performance. "It's like turning on the television set," says Wirthlin. "We leave it on all the time. We don't take our finger off the pulse."[14]

In the mid-1970s Wirthlin also began using the technique of simulations to develop predictive models for political strategy. This allows the team to run a variety of "what if?" scenarios before and during the campaign, reacting in advance to possible moves by the opposing candidates, possible developments on the international scene, possible changes in the stock market, or possible outcomes of TV debates. Having in place a variety of futuristic scenarios and countermoves helps keep the campaign on top of developing action.

While Wirthlin was perfecting his polling techniques with an eye towards the 1980 presidential race, a few other changes were occurring on the U.S. scene, changes that would help boost pollsters to a place of (back-stage) prominence. First, corporate business had gotten fed up with its dismally low "honest-ratings" in the polls, blaming them on a hostile press. Mobil Oil, in 1971, was the first to take decisive PR action. The weapon of choice was the advocacy ad based on attitudinal survey findings and designed to address demographic constituencies without going through the filter of adversarial reporters.

Second, in the mid-1970s the U.S. Census, a division of the Department of Commerce, developed a service that sold complex demographic data about the population to polling companies like Wirthlin's DMI. The data filled in whatever gaps existed in Wirthlin's PINS system, and opened up a new national data base for market researchers and pollsters across the country.[15]

   Third, in 1976 the U.S. Supreme Court ruled that political candidates could spend unlimited personal money on their campaigns,
and that "unaffiliated groups" could finance their pet candidates
without any restrictions on spending – as long as their activity was
not authorized by the candidate's official party organization. As a
result, special-interest groups quickly began forming their own
"political action committees" (PACs) to lobby for their own private
agendas and to finance political campaigns. As Joseph Fanelli, president of the powerful Business-Industry PAC, stated early in the
game: "We're interested in electing people with the right philosophy." (Between 1976 and 1982 PAC funding for candidates jumped
from $22.6 million to $80 million. By 1986 the figure had soared to
$342 million, with the average U.S. political candidate for office
receiving more than three times as much money from PACs as from
a party organization.)[16]

   This, then, was the political scene that greeted Allan Gregg during his 1978 tour of the top U.S. political pollsters and advisors. It
was all a vile travesty of real democracy; but, as Hunter S. Thompson would say, these things happen. And behind the scenes, busily
gathering data on the vulnerable citizen psyche, was the pollster,
whose psychographic profiles provide the basis for fine-tuning every
political and corporate marketing strategy.

   As Allan Gregg could no doubt see, there was nothing quite like it
in Canada. The first step was to erect a decent polling apparatus,
since tracking, especially daily tracking, was the key to every successful campaign.

□

In the late 1970s another busy Canadian was also impressed with
Wirthlin's work. Tom Scott of Sherwood Communications, an ad-
exec and top honcho among the Ontario Tories, had quickly sized up
the polling inadequacies of Bob Teeter and decided that it should be
possible to build a Canadian polling company to operate in the private market and also be on call to the Conservative party.

   He talked to Wirthlin and the two agreed to start up a fifty-fifty
joint-venture company in Canada, Decima Research Ltd. Sherwood
Communications would provide the start-up money, and Wirthlin's
DMI the state-of-the-art computer technology, polling methodolo-
gies, and expertise. While the deal was being struck, Scott convinced
Wirthlin that Allan Gregg would be a worthwhile partner, not only

because of his obvious abilities but also to avoid that old "Bob Teeter syndrome" wherein a U.S. pollster was running the show. Wirthlin agreed, and Gregg was cut in with a one-fifth share.[17]

Wirthlin moved his vice-president of administration from California to Toronto and sent a technical wizard to get all the hardware – the big phone banks and the computers – up and operating. There was also the necessary business of tutoring Gregg. Wirthlin was the ideal mentor and Gregg was the ideal student, with an innate flair for the subtleties and intricacies of the polling business. As Gregg later observed, "No one can analyze data faster than I can. I just crunch it up."[18] Very soon Wirthlin was assuring his eager student about his prospects, that he would soon be "the number-one pollster in the country". Decima opened for business in July 1979, sporting the most sophisticated hardware, software, and expertise that the country had ever seen. Meanwhile, Wirthlin had a little job to do back home. The polls were showing that people felt his presidential candidate-client might just nuke everything in sight once in office.

Decima did $800,000 of business in the first year, $1.8 million in the second, and $2.4 million in the third. Despite this healthy growth, investors lost half a million dollars. Part of the loss came from Decima's financing of *The Decima Quarterly*, a report of research survey findings sold by subscription to corporate and governmental marketers for $24,000 a year. No doubt modeled after the similar quarterly developed in the United States by Patrick Caddell (private and Democratic Party pollster), Gregg's publication provided the attitudinal survey results of polls conducted every March, June, September, and December. By conducting in-depth polling interviews with fifteen hundred Canadians four times a year, *The Decima Quarterly* gave marketers and public-relations professionals a useful psychographic profile of changing attitudes, insecurities, values, and beliefs on a wide range of topics. Crucial for the area of PR called issues management, part of public affairs, the data helped to indicate the most resonant language choices and imagery useful in media-relations strategy and advertising.

In the first three years of Decima's operation there were only two subscribers for the *Quarterly*, thus making it a massive drain on the company's resources (since polling is a labour-intensive operation). But Gregg's idea was simply ahead of its time for Canada. As Sawatsky writes, summarizing Gregg's thinking:

The *Quarterly* could revolutionize public-affairs consulting. Used perceptively, it could give subscribers an inside peek into government thinking, since Ottawa spent big money measuring public opinion and studied the secret results carefully. The data – if published – would reveal the forces and restraints facing the bureaucracy on every major issue and allow lobbyists to figure out government's agenda, removing much of the hunch, guess and gossip from government relations. The *Quarterly* would be the next best thing to reading government's own confidential polls. For the first time the client could see the total environment the government saw.[19]

History proved Gregg right: by 1985 there were fifty-two subscribers, together paying over $1 million per year for the publication. Nonetheless, during the early years both Wirthlin and Sherwood Communications decided to sell their shares in the company to Kinburn Capital, a holding company involved with Public Affairs International Ltd., better known as PAI.

At the time, PAI was Decima's research partner for the *Quarterly* and a fast-rising PR company specializing in government relations for corporate clients, including lobbying in advance of legislation and policy measures. In 1983 the feasibility (and efficiency) of a company comprised of a psychographic-polling arm (Decima) and a public-affairs consulting specialist (PAI) was evident to everyone. PAI president David MacNaughton, PAI vice-president Michael Robinson, and Decima chair Allan Gregg bought back Decima and PAI from Kinburn Capital. It was a very smart move. By 1985 the PAI-Decima partnership was pulling in $17 million annually, as Canadian businesses began to recognize the usefulness and necessity of lobbying in a more concerted and organized way, as well as taking steps in issues-management campaigns based on the polls.

By 1984 the federal election revealed the benefits of Gregg's polling apparatus for the Tories, especially his ability to do daily tracking throughout a campaign, while the opposition pollsters limped behind with their weekly and / or spot-polling procedures. As Gregg says, "Daily tracking is very important for picking up the edge on things like policy and news management. But it's really important for organizational purposes. I can do five hundred interviews per night during a campaign. Over five nights that gives me a huge sample size – twenty-five hundred interviews all within the same sample frame." This work, presumably, provides a complete picture of what's happening in the minds of people across the country, riding by riding. "Tracking is basic for fine-tuning an election-projection model," says Gregg. Business also noted this distinctive feature of Decima, which was far in advance of any other polling outfit in Canada.

During the same year another change occurred that would become significant to later developments. As the result of an appeal under the Charter of Rights by the ultra-conservative National Citizens' Coalition, the section of the Canada Elections Act which had previously controlled activities and spending by special-interest groups was struck down. Spending by political parties and candidates remained limited by law, but there was no longer any curb on spending by special-interest groups, nor were they under any obligation to disclose the sources of their financing.

Thus by the mid-1980s a number of significant factors had come together in Canada: the rise of a highly sophisticated polling apparatus connected to the ruling Tory government, the rise of advocacy advertising as a way of bypassing the reportorial filter, the rise of corporate public-affairs PR as an organized way of influencing government behind closed doors, and the dismantling of that section of the Elections Act which had formerly controlled spending by special-interest groups. If to some this all looked like a simulacrum of earlier events in the United States, to a great extent it was.

But the situation was perfect for ramming through a free trade deal that had been discussed behind closed doors since at least 1982. Election '88, fought on the issue of free trade, became, in the words of reporter Nick Fillmore, "the largest lobbying and public relations effort in Canadian history".[20] At the centre of the melee, during a campaign in which one out of four voters changed their minds at least once, was Tory pollster Allan Gregg.

□

"I've done thirty campaigns on three continents," says Gregg, "and I have never, ever been in a campaign where a trend started, stopped and reversed. Normally, when campaigns fall apart, they really fall apart."[21] The "trend" Gregg is referring to was the nine-point drop in the polls experienced by the Conservative Party after the TV debates (October 24-25). The party went into the debates with a seemingly secure first place (40 per cent of decided voters). But the following day pollster Martin Goldfarb announced that "40 per cent of the electorate is prepared to change its mind in the current election". As that change of mind began to show up in Gregg's daily tracking, Tory popularity was taking a nose-dive, indicating that their campaign was indeed "falling apart".

This trend obviously hinged on a change in public perception with regard to free trade's impact on Canada's sovereignty, especially its social programs. Gregg believes that before the TV debates two-thirds of the electorate simply did not believe that free trade jeopardized Canadian health care, unemployment insurance benefits, old-age pensions, or day care. "We knew if they did believe it," says Gregg, "the pins under free trade would get kicked out very quickly."

The Mulroney government's $24-26 million free trade "information" campaign, buttressed by a $3 million advocacy ad campaign conducted by the Canadian Alliance for Trade and Job Opportunities from March 1987 onwards, had led the pro-free-trade forces to assume that the deal was in the bag. But in the last weeks of October two events occurred that challenged that assumption. The Pro-Canada Network – an anti-free-trade umbrella organization representing labour groups, church groups, environmental groups, and provincial coalitions – distributed a booklet called "What's the Big Deal?" in twenty newspapers across Canada. The booklet challenged the governmental and business sector whitewash on free trade, raising the deeper issues and implications of the deal. Similarly, the TV debates put the issues of sovereignty and social programs squarely before the public in the charged and emotional exchanges between candidates.

If before, for much of the Canadian public, the free trade deal had seemed a primarily beneficial agreement, these two events knocked a "legitimacy gap" into the deal that was big enough to drive the Liberal Party through. In the two weeks following the debates the Liberals gained fourteen points in the polls, soaring from third to first place. Voter reaction to the debates caught PC strategists completely off guard. When the electorate's change of mind began to show up immediately in Gregg's daily tracking, the blood pressure in the Tory camp started to skyrocket in direct inverse correlation to the plunging Tory popularity. Says Gregg, "These guys, the Tories, were absolutely, utterly, morally outraged."[22] That outrage soon found a key target.

In analysing the Liberal resurrection taking place after October 26, Tory strategists concluded that at least half of the Liberals' impressive point-gains in the polls was coming from a category of the electorate referred to in back-room parlance as "the open-minded confused" – that portion of voters which, according to the Tories, was primarily made up of "inner-city, blue-collar workers, housewives, and the elderly".[23] Members of this group were considered to be confused about the merits of free trade, believing that it might hurt Canada's sovereignty, but also that it might help the country's growth economically. To keep the Mulroney campaign from falling apart completely, the pro-free-trade forces decided to concentrate their efforts on winning over the "open-minded confused", which the Tories believed constituted some 30 per cent of the electorate.

As well, Decima was doing some frenzied psychographic polling to determine how respondents perceived John Turner, asking if they believed that Turner was truly opposed to free trade or was using free trade to save his campaign. Initially, 55 per cent of the respondents said that Turner was sincere in opposing the deal, while 40 per cent doubted his motives.[24] On the basis of this polling data, says Gregg, "We saw that the bridge that joined the growing fear of free trade and the growing support for the Liberal Party was John Turner's credibility. So we had to get all the planes in the air and smash the bridge and blow it up."[25]

One of the first in the pro-free-trade sector to pick up on the full implications of the TV debates was Peter Lougheed, co-chair of the Canadian Alliance for Trade and Job Opportunities (referred to here-after as the Alliance). When the morning-after polls indicated that 72 per cent of the populace felt Turner had won the debate, Lougheed's speech of October 26 to the Retail Council of Canada hinted at the necessary tone for the remainder of the campaign. "I want Canadians to play the game recognizing that nice guys finish last," he told his audience, knowing that his words would likely gain headlines the following day.[26] Though the context of the remark was the way to conduct business in an open market, the co-chair of the Alliance was nevertheless addressing more immediate concerns.

Meanwhile, the sudden stress was taking its toll on Mulroney's media-grooming. On October 28th, at a rally in Kingston when he and Flora MacDonald were booed by a large group of anti-free-trade protesters, Mulroney shouted back: "Any time, any time ... I'll take you on any time. Flora and me!" When the heckling continued he retaliated, "I'll tell you what my mother would do with you! She'd wash your mouth out with soap!"[27]

It was a pathetic moment, and the Tory strategists and image doctors must have blanched in horror. Scrambling frantically to save the plunging Tory campaign, Canada's business sector realized it was crucial to get some Real Men out on the campaign trail. Following Lougheed's subtle advice about the fate of "nice guys", John Crosbie, Michael Wilson, Jake Epp, Don Mazankowski, and Simon Reisman were soon out on the hustings, slinging he-man insults and going into hyper-gear with the jabbing forefinger. In the midst of the torrent of rhetoric about "liars", "traitors", "scare-mongers", "cowards", and "wimps", it was apparent that the whole basis of the campaign had moved away from the details of free trade and over to an entirely different footing, so to speak. Asked after the election about the tactics that were used, Marcel Coté, a member of the PC team, said, "We planted the words 'liar' and 'incompetent', and, well, it worked."[28]

Assisted by the Wilson-Crosbie-Epp-Mazankowski-Reisman role models, Mulroney got back into the Real Man saddle. In assessing the opposition Mulroney referred to the NDP's Svend Robinson, a declared homosexual, with a sniggering remark at a November 2 rally. "Wouldn't that be something," he snickered, "Svend as minister of defence. I'll tell ya that would make one fine ministerial meeting." The remark went over so well that he used it again the next day at another rally. When reporters later suggested to him that he had made a slur, Mulroney coolly answered, "So what?"[29]

Simultaneously, Tom Scott, chairman of Toronto's Sherwood Capital Inc. and in charge of the PC English-language ad campaign, had created some new TV and radio ads questioning Turner's competence. Placement of these ads apparently coincided with data about the viewing habits of the "open-minded confused". Says Gregg, "We bought 'The Young and the Restless', we were in 'Romper Room'."[30] Under the Canada Elections Act, political advertising can take place only during the last four weeks of a federal election (advertising, that is, by the parties). The Act's complicated formula for allocating free and paid advertising space, based partially on political standings and the number of seats being contested, gave the Tories a distinct advantage over the Liberals and the NDP. They were allocated 195 minutes of paid airtime, compared with 89 minutes for the Liberals and 67 minutes for the NDP.[31] By November 4 the redesigned Tory ads were ready.

In those crucial days immediately following the debates, the pro-free-trade special-interest groups were also scurrying madly to reverse the disastrous trends in the polls. Roger Hamel, president of the Canadian Chamber of Commerce, sent out a letter to the Chamber's 170,000 member corporations across the country, urging them to promote free trade by "calling employees together to talk to them" and by making public speeches and writing the newspapers. The Canadian Manufacturers' Association sent letters to its three thousand member companies, similarly urging them to engage in some emergency labour-relations efforts about the merits of the deal and to voice support locally. When questioned by the press about such employer pressure on workers, the Chamber of Commerce's Hamel responded: "I think it's an absolutely vital development. You're going to see a lot more exchange of information. It's part of the healthy evolution in improving employer-employee relations."[32]

The Manitoba Committee for Free Trade spent $60,000 on TV, radio, and newspaper ads endorsing free trade during those crucial nine days, and the Ontario Chamber of Commerce urged its powerful membership to become more active on the issue. The National Citizens' Coalition spent $200,000 on advocacy newspaper ads, and $500,000 on two new ads to air on eight hundred radio and ninety TV stations across the country. Tory strategists came out with a new tabloid entitled "The Ten Big Lies of the Debates" for distribution by canvassers. And, not to be outdone, the Alliance – having already spent $3 million promoting free trade before the TV debates – quickly raised, in less than two weeks, another $2 million. On November 1 the Alliance announced that it was about to launch a four-page newspaper advocacy campaign entitled "Straight Talk on Free Trade", a $1.5-million PR campaign to be published in thirty-five newspapers across the country on November 3.

"It's not a panic move," said Thomas d'Aquino, member of the Alliance's executive committee, during the November 1 press conference. According to the published polls, however, the Tories were still sliding downward on November 1. Explained d'Aquino, "The fear-mongering on the other side has increased substantially. It's important to get the facts out there." Referring to the Pro-Canada Network's booklet "What's the Big Deal?", d'Aquino said its charges that free trade threatens Canadian social programs, culture, and sovereignty "are pretty strong stuff.... We felt the responsible thing to do was to counter with a dissimilar initiative and not with cartoons of ridicule and all sorts of incredible and unfounded statements."[33]

In response to this Alliance move, Mel Hurtig, spokesperson for the Pro-Canada Network (which by this point had exhausted most of its $815,000 budget), charged on November 1 that much of the $2 million raised by the Alliance in the preceding weeks (and indeed much of its $5 million campaign overall) had come from U.S. companies. As reported in *The Chronicle Herald* on November 2, Hurtig charged that U.S. branch-plant backers of the Alliance "have a vested interest in pushing the agreement, since it will allow them to buy up more of Canada and control more industry, resources and agriculture in this country".

Alliance spokesperson Lorne Walls (PR manager for Alcan) retaliated the following day, informing the press that between the time the Alliance was formed (March 1987) and September 1, 1988, it had received a total of $2.99 million from 131 "financial supporters". "This does not include small, individual donations," said Walls. "Of those 131 donors, 23 are multinational corporations, such as Sears Canada Inc. and General Electric Canada Inc. The other 108 are pure Canadian companies."

"I don't care how many times they deny [it]," Hurtig told *The Globe and Mail* (November 3), "the vast majority of their funds comes directly from membership of the Business Council on National Issues."

Peter Lougheed, co-chair of the Alliance (who shares duties with Donald Macdonald, ex-commissioner of the "leap of faith" Macdonald Royal Commission on the Economy), explained the same day, in answer to Hurtig's charges, that he was not privy to the Alliance's fund-raising information "but I would not be involved if it was just big business. It's made up of independent business people and the Canadian Association of Chambers of Commerce. It's a broadly based Alliance with support from chambers such as Trochu (a small town in Alberta). That's definitely not big business." Nevertheless, the ability to raise $2 million in less than two weeks suggested that either the good people of towns like Trochu were all quickly mortgaging their houses to finance the Alliance, or there were some major corporate high-rollers feeding money into its coffers.

□

Under the Canada Election Act, spending by political parties and
candidates is limited by law. But, thanks to the National Citizens'
Coalition, there is no curb on spending by special-interest groups,
nor are they under any obligation to disclose the sources of their
financing. "The act to control election expenses," states George
Allen, commissioner of elections, "was meant to allow access to politics to everyone, not just the rich and powerful, and to have some
accountability for the money that's spent. It seems to have fallen
apart a bit."

The Alliance had indicated on October 6, when it released its
latest pro-free-trade advocacy campaign, that it was going to publish
the names of contributors and their donations immediately. As the
weeks went by and no list was forthcoming, Hurtig challenged the
Alliance on November 2 to publish its donors list as proof that its
financing was not coming from U.S. corporate backers.

By November 3 the Alliance had done a reversal on its former
pledge. "Yes, I'm backtracking," spokesperson Lorne Walls told the
press. "You can blame me for that."

But just as funding of the pro-free-trade Alliance was about to
become an issue in the campaign – and possibly an issue that could
send the Tories into an even deeper nose-dive in the polls – a surprise
move occurred on November 3, the same day that Hurtig's charges
were appearing in most of the mainstream media.

By a simple twist of fate, coinciding with a new low in Tory polling, former chief justice of the Supreme Court of Canada Emmett
Hall, "the father of Medicare", stepped forward. Stating that he was
acting entirely on his own initiative, Hall proposed that Turner and
Broadbent "were not being truthful about what is in this [free trade]
document".

On November 3 Hall told the press that there was no basis for
arguments that a provision of the deal covering management services of health-care facilities means that U.S. companies will be able
to run private hospitals in Canada. He said that the clause "simply
refers to the provision of items such as food services by outside companies and not health care. This type of thing is quite common
across Canada, so there is nothing new dealing with the control of
hospitals".

Clearly the honourable former chief justice must have neglected to read the fine print in the deal, especially the list of 299 service industries whose management was to be opened to U.S. private companies under free trade. That list of services includes (in "Division P – Health and Social Service Industries") management of virtually every type of hospital, health clinic, nursing home, and community health centre, as well as medical labs and blood banks.

Nonetheless when questioned by the press, including CBC-Radio's "As It Happens", Emmett Hall was an effective and affective voice for winning over the "open-minded confused". "I'm here to tell you there is nothing in this agreement damaging to medicare in Canada," he stated. "If I had found there was in this free trade agreement provisions which would damage medicare or would destroy it ... I would have opposed the agreement because medicare is perhaps one of the things I hold dearest in life today."

It was an obvious stroke of luck for the pro-free-trade forces. "The game is up as far as these falsehoods [from Turner and Broadbent] are concerned," railed Crosbie on CTV's "Canada A.M." on November 4, "because people are coming forward like the former Chief Justice Hall, the father of medicare, who says this doesn't affect medicare." Meanwhile the Alliance's "Straight Talk on Free Trade" campaign, released on the same day as Hall's statements, gained credibility from his words, which did not contradict this passage in the four-page ad:

> WHAT ABOUT OUR SOCIAL PROGRAMS LIKE PENSIONS AND MEDICARE? The Free Trade Agreement is about trade. Period. Not social programs, not culture, not the environment. These are not traded commodities. Services such as health and welfare, day care, education and public administration are not in the agreement and are not threatened in any way by it. In fact, nothing in the agreement prevents Canada from maintaining or expanding programs in any of these vital areas.

The events of November 3 added significant fuel to the Wilson-Crosbie-Epp-Mazankowski-Reisman-Mulroney fulminations about "scare-mongering" by opposition "liars".

In their post-election analysis (*The Financial Post*, November 28) Tory strategists described Emmett Hall's statements as being "perhaps most important" to the Tory assault on Turner's credibility and to the subsequent shift in voter perception regarding free trade. In addition they noted that the Alliance's November 3 advocacy campaign "contributed to the growing perception Turner had overstated his case". For these reasons, Tory pollster Allan Gregg says he knew by November 4 that the Tory campaign, and the trade deal, had been saved. That frenzied nine-day blitz of activity following the TV debates was starting to register in his daily tracking. During that period Gregg's sample of five hundred attitudinal interviews per night meant that by day nine he could make projections on the basis of 4,500 polled households – a highly useful strategy not only for gauging the timing and placing of ads, photo-ops, and other campaign tactics, but also for determining the best language and imagery to utilize in any emergency PR strategy.

For example, one of the sub-themes in the Tories' "issues management" tactics was the credibility of the opposition's understanding of the deal's implications. Free trade negotiator Simon Reisman had attacked the "amateur" analysis of the trade deal "from every Tom, Dick, and Marjorie" – a reference to retired judge Marjorie Bowker's popular text *On Guard for Thee* containing a clause-by-clause analysis of the deal, and Marjorie Cohen's book *Free Trade and the Future of Women's Work*. Similarly, the Alliance's "Straight Talk on Free Trade" four-page ad was purposely designed to look sober and authoritative by contrast to the Pro-Canada Network's "cartoons of ridicule" (in D'Aquino's words). This sub-theme may well have been based on Gregg's psychographic surveying, finding the right tone in which to address the "open-minded confused".

That authoritative and paternalistic tone characterized the rest of the campaign and was reflected in the torrent of advocacy ads that blanketed the media in the closing weeks. For example, on November 16 a full-page pro-free-trade ad appearing in many of Canada's newspapers stated that it was "sponsored for the concerned employees of these Canadian companies: Don Park Inc.; Minto Construction Ltd.; Harris Steel Group; Green Forest Lumber Corp.; CEECO Machinery Mfg. Ltd.; INDUCON Group of Companies". "Don't be deceived by political showmanship, scare tactics and bombastic humbug" stated the bold print, adding at the end: "For your free copy of an unbiased, detailed evaluation of Free Trade, you may call the Canadian Alliance for Trade and Job Opportunities."

Similarly, a November 18 full-page ad placed by Rayrock Yellowknife Resources Inc. in many newspapers stated the prevailing pro-free-trade advocacy tone: "For Canada's sake, make an informed decision. Listen to the experts if you're confused by the politicians." The ad mentioned three experts, including Emmett Hall and University of Toronto professor Alan Rugman. But the first expert listed was Thomas d'Aquino, identified as "President and CEO of the Business Council on National Issues". Neglecting to mention d'Aquino's membership in the Executive Committee of the Alliance, the ad ended by saying: "We have listened to the experts and reviewed the facts. We urge you to do the same."

Meanwhile, as Nick Fillmore has documented, the Alliance was on a huge PR spending spree during the last three weeks of the campaign.

> An additional 200,000 copies of the newspaper insert were printed and distributed by member groups of the alliance. It spent several thousand dollars renting electronic billboards along busy roads in Toronto and Hamilton. The day before the election, a plane rented by the alliance flew over Toronto's Exhibition Stadium, where the Grey Cup game was being played, carrying a banner that read: "Free Trade Builds Canada". The alliance also spent $65,000 on five full-page ads in the *Financial Post* during the last week of the campaign, and $75,000 on a five-page insert in *Maclean's* that arrived at the homes of 600,000 subscribers the Friday before the election. To give an appearance of some degree of balance, *Maclean's*, whose owners supported free trade, donated two pages of advertising in the same issue to the Pro-Canada Network. However, the alliance ad had a prime location toward the front of the magazine, between interviews with Mulroney and Turner, while the Pro-Canada ad was buried in the world coverage section toward the back.[34]

At the same time this spending spree was on in full force, Mulroney's advisors began to turn his October 28th glitch about his mother and the soap into a recurring photo-op. Visiting the senior citizens' club at Kiwanis Place Lodge in Edmonton, Mulroney spoke on November 4th about the opposition "demagoguery" on the campaign trail, giving his assurances that "No one is going to take away your pensions or medical services." Invoking the name of his mother Irene, Mulroney explained that she was in a similar facility in Montreal. "I feel very much as if I am speaking in the company of friends of my own mother," he said. "If she were here, I'd say, 'Ma, your pension is okay, your medicare is okay'." By November 13th it was time to pose for the cameras, with Irene at his side (*sans* soap), saying "Never would I sign an accord that would have the effect of threatening my own mother's old-age pension and social pensions." As Gregg and other Tory strategists had advised, the elderly were a significant target audience in the "open-minded confused".

Fillmore convincingly documents that "the pro-free trade forces spent about six-and-a-half million dollars during the last three weeks of the election campaign. The anti-freetraders could raise less than one million dollars. During the two-year period leading up to the election, it's estimated that the pro-free trade forces spent more than $56 million promoting their deal while anti-trade groups probably spent about five million dollars – that's a spending ratio of about ten to one."[35]

If it took $56 million to close the legitimacy gap around the free trade deal there must be some serious problems with it, though getting that news to the public depended a great deal on the politics of media relations, as well as on media conventions.

For example, the Canadian Environmental Law Association (CELA) did a careful study of the environmental repercussions of the deal and mounted a press conference in late September to explain these issues. This event was well reported, but in retrospect it's clear that the timing of it worked badly. When the last four weeks of the campaign were in full swing, with the issue now switched to the "credibility" of not just Turner and Broadbent but all opposition experts, CELA fell victim to one of the prevailing conventions of news. It is not possible to call another press conference and reiterate information already released, no matter how pertinent that information is to the debate; thus CELA's expert analysis was "old news" and not, to my knowledge, referred to again in the press.

Similarly, there was no accounting for taste in the "objective" mainstream media during the campaign. Scott Sinclair of the Pro-Canada Network told Fillmore that *The Globe and Mail* was "the worst" paper of all when it came to biased reporting on both the pros and cons of free trade. "There's no question about it," Sinclair said. As a traditionally Tory paper and part of the Thomson media conglomerate, *The Globe* went all out in support of free trade. Sinclair also found the CBC, especially "The National", guilty of "bad" reporting on the issue. "I could build a case and show how we took story after story to them that they didn't report. When we held a news conference to announce our free trade booklet, we couldn't get the CBC or anyone to come and cover it. But later, when the alliance held a press conference to announce it was running an insert in papers across the country, there was extensive coverage." Sinclair singled out the CBC's attack on John Turner as worthy of special note in the pro-free-trade campaign.[36]

□

Perhaps the most interesting aspect of the mainstream media's campaign coverage was its overwhelming silence about the connection between the Alliance and the Business Council on National Issues (BCNI). On November 7, four days after Hurtig's charges regarding the Alliance's multinational funding and its connection to the BCNI, the Consumers' Association of Canada dropped out of the Alliance, charging it with "partisan politics" and claiming "it's a business lobby". Nevertheless, a great media silence fell over the BCNI-Alliance connection, indicating (as press silence often does) the political sensitivity surrounding that partnership. Indeed, even after the election was over *Maclean's* (December 5) perpetuated the mystification in its post-election wrap-up by reporting: "In response [to the Pro-Canada Network], the large pro-free trade business community in Canada countered by creating a loosely defined organization called the Canadian Alliance for Free Trade and Job Opportunities — representing 35 companies and business associations — and spent an estimated $1.5 million on its own ad campaign."[37]

Nick Fillmore estimates that this "loosely defined organization" spent $6 million before and during the campaign on pro-free-trade PR, and, as well, it managed to establish itself as the source of "expert opinion" on the deal. But what the general public was never, to my knowledge, informed about during the campaign was the fact that the Alliance was the creation of the BCNI, which provided the direction and the money. Political economist David Langille, who wrote extensively for the alternative press about the BCNI both before and during the election campaign, stated, "The BCNI recruited Peter Lougheed and Donald Macdonald to co-chair the Alliance, while BCNI Chairman David Culver is the chair of the Executive Committee behind the Alliance's advocacy ad campaigns."[38] Thomas d'Aquino, president and CEO of the BCNI, was serving on the Executive Committee of the Alliance before and during the election.

The reason this BCNI-Alliance connection would have been an

important story during the election is that the BCNI, "a virtual shadow cabinet" in Langille's view, has since 1986 recommended that the federal government cut spending on social programs. As the most powerful public-affairs lobby group in the country, the BCNI (which represents 150 blue-chip corporations) advised the government in its *Social Policy Reform and the National Agenda*: "Although many of Canada's social programs have by and large worked quite well in the past, new demographic, economic and fiscal challenges suggest that the time has come to consider seriously how they might be made more effective.... Major reforms are required in several principal areas of social policy."[39]

The key areas targeted by the BCNI in 1986 for "major reforms" were: family benefits, unemployment insurance benefits, old-age pensions, health-care spending, and university funding. The BCNI recommended that the federal government make budgetary cuts in every category and utilize "greater selectivity" of benefits recipients. Mulroney was echoing the tenor of this BCNI social policy document when, during the TV debates, he stated that "I think the best social program is a job".

In its call for "major reforms" and "selectivity" in Canada's universal social programs, the 1986 BCNI document argues that it is acting through a sense of "social realism" about the annual $55 million spent by the federal government on social programs. A better explanation can be found (ironically enough) in the Alliance's November 3 advocacy ad "Straight Talk on Free Trade":

SOME CRITICS MAY CHARGE THAT UNDER THE FREE TRADE AGREEMENT, AMERICANS COULD TARGET OUR SOCIAL PRO-GRAMS AS AN "UNFAIR SUBSIDY". According to the international trade law and practice under GATT (General Agreement on Tariffs and Trade) *programs which are universally available cannot be considered an unfair subsidy.* Programs such as Medicare, Unemployment Insurance, the Canada Pension Plan and Family Allowance are available to all Canadians. They cannot be deemed as subsidies, and therefore they simply are not at risk. [My emphasis.]

The BCNI's 1986 recommendations to make Canada's social programs more "selective" and better "targeted" might thereby make those programs no longer universally available to all Canadians. They could therefore become, under the terms of GATT, "unfair subsidies" – the necessary step for eliminating them altogether.

In this context it should also be noted that another BCNI document, its 1987 Defence Paper entitled "National Security and International Responsibility", recommends increases in federal military spending of 4 to 6 per cent annually until the year 2000, to be financed by reallocating resources from existing government programs.

Thus the BCNI-Alliance connection should have been a major issue in the campaign but, to my knowledge, it received nothing but silence from the mainstream media. A quick scan of the BCNI membership as of 1986 (provided as a public service in the Appendix) suggests a few reasons for that silence. The BCNI membership includes not only Southam Inc., owner of many of Canada's major dailies, but also companies controlled by press magnate Thomson. As well, most of the BCNI member corporations are major buyers of ad time and space in the mainstream media. They who pay the piper call the tune.

As the most powerful special interest group in the country, the BCNI has task forces that influence every area of government. According to Langille, "Their task forces cover the areas of national finance, international economy and trade, taxation, competition policy, energy policy and natural resources, federal-provincial relations, social policy and retirement income, labour relations and manpower, government organization and regulation, foreign policy and defence, education, and corporate governance."

"We'll be around as long as there is a need for us," stated the Alliance's Lorne Walls on December 17, 1988, adding that the group's work would probably continue for several years. "We will counsel and assist our members on how to make announcements concerning free trade," he said. Thus the Alliance planned to co-ordinate press releases, press conferences, and all the other media-relations strategies in order to "accentuate the positive" in the midst of plant closings, lay-offs, and other free trade fallout.

Meanwhile Mulroney's five-member Adjustment Panel, touted as "the best protector of Canadian workers hit by free trade", is chaired by BCNI member Jean de Grandpré, whose own company, Northern Telecom, was one of the first to announce plant closings after the November 21 election. But as BCNI Chairman David Culver put it, workers who suffer under free trade "are like flowers that die so that other flowers can grow. You can't have growth in the garden without some deaths." The day after the votes were cast Culver crowed, "I think this whole campaign will tend to make business a bigger player in the whole field of public policy than before." Apparently running a "shadow cabinet" isn't enough for the BCNI. They want to run it all.

And they very likely will, given some subsequent developments. Part of the fallout of that '88 election was an obvious flurry of corporate take-overs and mergers, leading to some mighty large corporate bodies in that reverse fat-farm called free enterprise. Not to be outdone, Decima Research Ltd. has engaged in its own corporate moves – proving that it doesn't just merge data.

In February 1989 the Decima-PAI partnership was bought up by WPP, the huge parent company that owns two big ad agencies (J. Walter Thompson and Ogilvy) and the largest independent PR firm in the United States, Hill and Knowlton. Ironically enough, Hill and Knowlton's polling arm is Richard Wirthlin's DMI, meaning that the former mentor and investor has now taken over Gregg's outfit. And, of course, he's happy.

"As of the third week in February," says Gregg, "Decima, PAI – which specializes in government-relations – and Hill and Knowlton [which specializes in every form of public relations] are under the same roof. We are the only company in Canada which will now be able to deliver *full service* for a client."

"Does this mean you'll be designing advocacy ads?" I ask.

"This means doing advocacy ads, corporate image, speech-writing, contacts, media relations, news management, *full* service. The thing we heard most in the past was clients would say to us: 'We did all this [polling] research and then we didn't do something with it.' Now that has changed."

I can hear the excitement in Gregg's voice and I know why. Hill and Knowlton has been doing public-relations work for nearly sixty years and has a tremendous clientele world-wide: governments, multinationals, industry associations, political parties, you name it. "We are providers of services," Gregg is saying, "and they are looking at their suppliers to come with them." I tune out momentarily while he's talking. I've just remembered something else my Decima deep-throat told me: that attitudinal surveying is two-tiered. "During the week we survey the populace," Silkwood had said, "but on weekends a different staff comes in. They telephone individual corporate executives at home, by name, to get their attitudes and opinions on issues. That's a different data base."

You don't have to be Richard Wirthlin to guess what happens with *that* polling data. It helps to maintain accord and communications between corporate movers-and-shakers and policy-makers of the party in power. That, indeed, is the essence of public-affairs consulting: corporate PR to affect and impact on government planning and thinking in advance of decisions. With Hill and Knowlton under the same roof, Decima will be accessing corporate desires world-wide, as well as fine-tuning their PR strategies at every level. The merger facilitates that current PR buzzword, "one-stop shopping", whereby all of a client's public-relations needs can be met by one huge outfit that operates on an international, national, regional, and local level.

Thus the merger must be seen within the larger context of what, in the next chapter, is called the Multinational Free Lunch, a movable feast that has received new impetus during the late 1980s. Meanwhile, the pollsters will keep their earnest fingers on our psychographic pulse, registering every blip, dip, peak, and twist in our mind-set so that *full service* can be provided for clients. An awesome image arises in the mind: Richard Wirthlin's data bank, twenty years in the making, merging with all the accumulated psychographic data of Decima Research Ltd. Full service indeed.

5
Multinational Free Lunch:
The Zones That Eat the World

How many hours does a person work in a day? Here at the Viron Garments Factory, located in the Bataan Export Processing Zone in Mariveles, we work 16 hours a day, 7 days a week, without Sunday off or a rest day.

FILIPINA WORKER, Bataan EPZ

Free trade zones are like Hilton Hotels. When you're inside, you don't know what country you're in, and the hassles of the country don't touch you. It's a businessman's dream. And the workers are polite and obedient and almost look alike – sometimes you wonder if they're Mexicans, Filipinos, Malays or Arabs.

U.S. BUSINESSMAN, Seoul, South Korea

DURING HER SEPTEMBER 1986 visit to the United States, Philippines President Corazon Aquino was concerned that the recent "revolution" in her country might be wrongly perceived in certain important circles. Consequently a three-page advocacy ad appeared in *The New York Times* during her tour, announcing in bold print: "Aquino Welcomes Foreign Investors". Meanwhile her ambassador to the United States, Emmanuel Palaez, had been busy speaking at trade conferences and power breakfasts since May, touting "our relatively inexpensive but skilled labour" as an important selling point.[1] With eleven export processing zones (EPZs) dotting the country and easing the way for hundreds of multinational "offshore" operations, it was best that the Philippine revolution not be seen as *too* revolutionary.

In a park in Metro Manila there is a giant replica of a TV set erected on a pedestal: homage to all the foreign manufacturers, especially the electronics corporations, that have flocked to the Philippines EPZs since the mid-1970s, lured by the "relatively inexpensive" labour pool. The thousands of Filipina women who work in the zones earn an average of $100 U.S. per month — less than fifty cents an hour.

Many of them live in the shanty-towns that have sprung up by each EPZ, sleeping in hovels and buying drinking water from the roving water-sellers. After about four years of working in an EPZ assembly-plant — where health and safety standards are usually minimal and the work-week anywhere from 48 to 112 hours — an employee's health has often deteriorated to such a degree that she is considered unfit to continue. The next step might be joining the hundreds of thousands of prostitutes who service the fourteen U.S. military installations located throughout the Philippines. In Manila alone there are more than a hundred thousand prostitutes, who eat their lunches and rest in the park where the giant TV set towers overhead.

At the Bic Pen factory in the Bangkok free trade zone (FTZ), the Thai women workers assemble more than a hundred thousand ballpoint pens per day. If they do not meet their quotas they are subject to a fine. If they take more than twenty-five minutes break-time during an eight-hour shift they are penalized by the loss of bonuses. As one Thai zone worker writes, "The management think we are machines. Time is all important for them. We clock in and clock off and in between there is not even time to go to the toilet."[2] If the Thai FTZ workers are identified as "troublemakers" (read, union organizers) they can be fired. And if they complain about their average monthly salary of $64 U.S. they are reminded by management that there are a hundred applicants waiting in line for every job. As an employer in Thailand's free trade zone, Bic Pen Company does not have to abide by practices that workers in the First World take for granted.

For the eighty thousand women workers in Malaysia's four free trade zones, life isn't quite what the company recruiters sent to the villages said it would be. Dormitory housing provided in the zones consists of a ten-by-twelve-foot room for every six to ten workers: basically a cot and a small closet shelf. Some companies, operating on a twenty-four-hour per day work schedule, use the "hot bed" approach to housing: one bed for every three workers. As one employee vacates the bed to go to work, another comes off shift to use it. For such "housing" a Malaysian worker pays an average of $12 a month out of a wage package based on the rate of sixty cents an hour.

But by comparison with the women zone workers in Sri Lanka the Malaysian women (and even the Thai women) are relatively fortunate. In Sri Lanka's EPZ the average worker's salary is $35 U.S. per month – a starvation wage that has attracted dozens of multinationals from the United States, Japan, Britain, and Europe to set up offshore assembly-plants there. At the Esquire Industries Ltd. zone plant, for example, each Sri Lankan employee sews a quota of twenty pairs of "Gloria Vanderbilt" jeans per day, earning a monthly wage of $28.10 U.S. Meanwhile, each pair of designer jeans she produces sells on the North American market for about $40.00. Clearly there are some real corporate benefits to be made from EPZs and FTZs.

Export processing zones and free trade zones are the horrific underside of the expanding multinational economy and of most of our "labour-saving" devices and leisure products. They are also a vivid example of international PR at work on two levels: first, as an idea heavily promoted by First World lending institutions and corporations to Third World governments, and second, as a continuing forum for PR efforts to attract multinational clients to the zones. The historical process by which the Third World was sold this neo-colonizing scheme is a tale of lies and woe, PR, marketing and manipulation at the highest levels of so-called "free world" politics. Most important, the massive Third World debt that we read about so often is in many ways a direct result of the EPZs and FTZs set up during the 1960s and 1970s.

□

In the late 1950s many Third World countries began to adopt economic policies based on "import substitution" – a plan in which indigenous industries were to be established to produce goods formerly imported from the overdeveloped world. These policies held the potential for transforming a dependent economy into a self-sustaining one, especially in conjunction with land-reform plans intended to accompany indigenous industrialization to serve local markets.

Given the extensive landholdings of First World companies in the underdeveloped world, such thinking was unappealing and unacceptable to foreign interests. With an eye to revolutionary Cuba and the spectre of the "domino theory", these interests stepped in to advise alternative measures. In the early 1960s First World "experts" recommended that the policy of "import substitution" would be too slow a process for countries wanting to industrialize their economies and improve their living standards. Instead, they advised a policy of "export-oriented industrialization" as the best non-communist development model. As the head of the World Bank, Robert McNamara, stated: "Special efforts must be made in many countries to turn their manufacturing enterprises away from the relatively small markets associated with import substitution, and toward the much larger opportunities flowing from export promotion."[3]

According to the First World "experts", the best way for underdeveloped countries to attract "opportunities" was to set up an infrastructure that would entice foreign multinationals to invest in Third World development. That infrastructure was to take the form of special export-oriented manufacturing zones – ideally, close to airports to facilitate quick turnover in the assembly process. The products assembled in such zones would not be available to local markets (or to the workers who assembled them) but would be exported back to the First World for consumption. Nonetheless, it was said, the zones would lead to a "trickle-down" of the latest technologies and skills as well as to better foreign exchange rates for the host countries involved.

For countries leery of foreign domination, EPZs and FTZs were pitched as a way of geographically "containing" the economic experiment: a zone of 400 acres (like the Masan FTZ in South Korea) might employ 25,000 workers in the dozens of assembly-plants but be considered separate from the country at large.

During the 1960s the zone idea was heavily promoted through a massive public-relations effort by U.S.-dominated lending institutions, including the World Bank, the International Monetary Fund (IMF), the Asian Development Bank, the U.S. Agency for International Development (U.S. AID), and the United Nations Industrial Development Organization (UNIDO), as well as by institutions like the Ford Foundation and private banks. These organizations encouraged underdeveloped countries to borrow heavily in order to erect the zone infrastructures – buildings and assembly-plants, airports, utilities, worker housing, on-site customs and governmental offices, stores and roads – to entice offshore manufacturers to the zones. Providing such facilities on a low-rent or no-rent basis to multinational clients was considered a necessary part of creating a "favourable business climate".

While the World Bank advised "wage restraints" in such zones, UNIDO recommended that the host governments provide other financial incentives as well: corporate income tax exemptions for up to ten years; full repatriation of profits; complete exemptions from duties and taxes on equipment, raw materials, and components; preferential tariff rates; preferential financing and credit on new construction in the zones.

Although the idea for EPZs and FTZs must, in retrospect, be seen as essentially a First World corporate public-relations scam, it coincided historically with another U.S.-promoted development plan that made such zones seem "necessary" for many countries' survival.

During the early 1960s scientists employed by multinational agribusiness developed new strains of seeds called "high-yield varieties" (HYVs) that were hyped as part of a so-called "Green Revolution" to end world hunger. Heavily backed by the Rockefeller Foundation and the Ford Foundation, the Green Revolution was promoted throughout the Third World through a massive PR campaign, especially during the years of 1965-73.[4] Countries were encouraged to abandon traditional peasant farming methods and adopt the new HYV monoculture farming methods to produce cash crops that could be sold on the world market.

Such crops were highly dependent on massive pesticide, herbicide, and fertilizer use, all sold by the same companies that had developed the "miracle seeds": Imperial Chemicals Industries (ICI), Ciba-Geigy, Monsanto, Hoechst, Bayer, and Dow Chemical among others. But HYV cash crops also completely replaced the subsistence crops by which a given region had previously provided its own food base. As Susan George documents in *How the Other Half Dies*, the main "beneficiaries" of the Green Revolution hype were Mexico, India, Pakistan, Turkey, Afghanistan, Nepal, North Africa, Taiwan, the Philippines, and Sri Lanka, which turned over millions of acres to the new HYV wheat and rice strains. According to George, in many countries U.S. interests pushed the Green Revolution "as an alternative to land reform and to the social change reform would require".[5]

While increasing cash-crop yields for export, the new farming methods nevertheless threw millions out of work in rural areas of underdeveloped countries. For example, in Indonesia in 1967 rice HYVs were introduced which could be harvested only by First World machine technologies (duly sold by Massey-Ferguson et al.). Made redundant by the new technologies, which the big landowners quickly adopted, millions of people in rural Indonesia were forced to migrate to the cities to look for work. Similarly, peasant farmers across the Third World were forced into buying imported foodstuffs since the land had been replanted with monoculture cash crops for export.

Such massive disruption by agribusiness interests occurred throughout the underdeveloped world during the 1960s, mainly benefiting the multinationals of the First World and the landowner class of the Third World countries. As the influx of rural newly-unemployed hit the cities of the countries where the misnamed Green Revolution had been promoted and adopted, the idea of export processing zones and free trade zones was pitched by lending institutions as a "solution" to unemployment.

□

Caught in this double bind, Third World governments compete with one another to attract multinational clients to their zones. It is standard procedure to hire an independent First World public-relations firm to engage in image-creation and promotion, especially among the elite community of international high finance. While most zones have followed UNIDO's terms – offering generous tax concessions, customs exemptions, and preferential treatment to foreign companies in every area of doing business – there is a need for expertise to handle that delicate area that PR executives think of as "risk perception". One international public-relations specialist, Andrew Weil, based in New York, emphasizes the combination of "low risk" and quantifiable benefit necessary to entice multinational corporate investors.

A company that has a board of directors and stockholders cannot make gambling decisions in terms of their resources being expropriated or otherwise swallowed up by an unfriendly or hostile government coming in to that nation. And therefore, they must be terribly, terribly secure about it. The primary role of a PR firm taking on one of these countries is to be able to demonstrate the fact that an investor going there will be secure.[6]

As the case of Argentina during the reign of the Generals shows, the ways in which a foreign government goes about ensuring a "favour-able business climate" internally, vis-à-vis political dissent, is pretty much its own affair. Once the international community of high finance is convinced that "stability" has been achieved – especially that there is no risk of a "hostile" government coming to power – then the international public-relations campaign is a success. The goal, as in the Burson Marsteller campaign, is to reach those key tar-geted publics: "those who influence thinking, those who influence investments," and (when pertinent) "those who influence travel". As Weil puts it, more bluntly, "A nation must be looked upon as a product."[7] Like any product, the right image for it must be created. This is true as well for the export processing zones and free trade zones within Third World countries, which must compete to keep their multinational clients happy.

By the mid-1980s there were more than 120 such zones world-wide, in Malaysia, the Dominican Republic, the Philippines, Thai-land, Sri Lanka, Hong Kong, Indonesia, Mexico, South Korea, Taiwan, Singapore, Mauritius, Egypt, Bombay, Puerto Rico, Jamaica, Colombia, Tunisia, China, Brazil, Haiti, Guatemala, Kuala Lumpur. More recently free trade zones have been developed in Cameroon, Ghana, Kenya, Sierra Leone, Sudan, Zambia, Bangladesh, Pakistan, Costa Rica, St. Lucia, Venezuela, Cyprus, Malta, Romania, Yugoslavia, and Hungary. The zones go by a variety of names in vari-ous countries: "duty free zones", "investment promotion zones", "free export zones", "export development zones", "special eco-nomic zones", "duty free enterprise zones"; but the most common terms used are EPZs and FTZs. The conditions of work in most of these zones are so appalling that it would be more accurate to call them slave labour camps.

The dozens of factories in each zone are usually First World off-shore assembly-plants, part of "the global assembly-line" in which the most labour-intensive and polluting aspects of the entire product-assembly process are exported to be done by Third World workers, mainly women, who are preferred as a "docile" workforce. Most zone workers are women between the ages of fourteen and thirty-four.

The top First World multinationals now have factories and sub-contractors in these EPZs and FTZs, including such familiar names as Liptons, Bic, Unilever (Lever Brothers), Imperial Tobacco, Union Carbide, Singer Industries, Fairchild, Motorola, J.C. Penny, Sears Roebuck, Intel Corp., National Semiconductor (NS), ITT, IBM, Tandy, Signetics (Philips Corp.), Philco-Ford, Control Data, General Motors, RCA, General Electric, Zenith, National Cash Register (NCR), United Technologies, Hewlett-Packard, Texas Instruments, Atari, Mattel Toys, Sanyo, Sony, General Instruments, Puma, Adidat, and Gulf & Western. These companies have the zone-host countries "by the short hairs", to put it crudely. If a "favourable business climate" is not maintained they will pack up and move elsewhere, virtually overnight.

Part of that "favourable business climate" is an incredibly low or non-existent minimum wage, maintained in the zones by repressive government practices. The most recent comparative wage figures that I could find are from the July 1982 issue of *Voice of Women*.[8] The following rates refer to average *monthly* income (expressed in U.S. dollars) for workers in EPZs and FTZs: Sri Lanka, $35; Indonesia, $40; India, $55; China, $57; Thailand, $64; Malaysia, $100; Philippines, $100; Taiwan, $100; South Korea, $130; Singapore, $165; Hong Kong, $240.

In their 1983 book *Women in the Global Factory* Annette Fuentes and Barbara Ehrenreich provide a wages-per-hour breakdown for the electronics plants operating in seven EPZs: Indonesia, $0.19; Philippines, $0.48; Malaysia, $0.48; Taiwan, $0.53; South Korea, $0.63; Singapore, $0.79; Hong Kong, $1.15.[9] Figures for the more recent African EPZs and FTZs are unavailable, but, to compete with the other zones and attract multinational clients, they are probably comparable to Sri Lanka's going wage rate of ten cents an hour.

This characteristic feature of most Third World zones is used as a selling point by the PR firms contracted by the host governments. In preparing promotion kits for distribution to the high-finance community, in films and videos promoting the country of their governmental client, and in advocacy ads placed in major business publications, PR firms always place high emphasis on the cheap wages paid in the zones. The following collage of PR hype excerpted from a variety of sources reveals the extent to which labour exploitation is itself exploited as a public-relations vehicle:

Haiti: "For only one U.S. dollar she will gladly work for 8 hours for you, and several hundred of her able friends are waiting for you."

Egypt: "Egypt has a surplus of employable labour. In these inflationary times, Egypt retains its significant wage-cost advantage over many other developing countries."

Colombia: "Male and female workers are easily obtained due to the high rate of unemployment, rapid increase of population and the emigration from the rural areas to the cities."

Puerto Rico: "Your payroll dollars are 50% more productive in Puerto Rico than the total U.S. average."

Malaysia: "The manual dexterity of the Oriental female is famous the world over. Her hands are small and she works fast with extreme care. Who, therefore, could be better qualified by nature and inheritance to contribute to the efficiency of a bench-assembly production line than the Oriental girl?"[10]

In many instances, First World PR firms advise their government clients on a wide range of internal policies, including zone employment recruitment strategies and employee relations. In many EPZs and FTZs union organizing is forbidden and immediately crushed. In South Korea, for example, the penalty for leading a strike is seven years' imprisonment. Thus, repressive and right-wing governments collaborate with multinational interests to ensure that the zones maintain the "favourable business climate". In some zones "company unions" are formed that serve primarily as "window-dressing". Any national minimum-wage laws are usually bypassed in the zones, and such things as job security, employment benefits, sick leave, and paid holidays are virtually unheard-of.

For "vital" industries (such as electronics firms) a no-strike policy is permanently in place. Zone workers are often required to work thirty-six- and forty-eight-hour "stay-ins" in order to meet special production deadlines. According to Fuentes and Ehrenreich, "Management often provides pep pills and amphetamine injections to keep the women awake and working; some of the women have become addicts."[11] Moreover, to earn a subsistence wage most zone employees *must* work extensive overtime hours, well beyond the forty-five- to forty-eight-hour work-week considered standard in EPZs. In South Korea, Taiwan, Hong Kong, and the Philippines, zone workers typically put in hundred-hour weeks just to get by.

Zone employers have been known to fire women workers who get married, since single female employees are considered more malleable, less likely to struggle for things like maternity benefits, and more able to work the overtime "stay-ins" when necessary. Some companies, like Mattel Toys, have actually awarded prizes to women who undergo sterilization, which is considered the sign of a "dependable" company employee.[12]

Zone health and safety standards are minimal, especially in the garment factories and electronic plants that account for the greatest percentage of assembly work in EPZs and FTZs. Garment factories are usually unventilated and stiflingly hot, with poor lighting and inadequate (or no) toilet facilities. The workers must meet high quotas or face fines and lay-offs. Besides the ongoing stress of relentless work for next to no pay, the women suffer from respiratory ailments and brown-lung caused by textile dust and lint. While the dampness inside the factories is useful for preserving thread, it causes rheumatism and arthritis even among the young workers employed.

Electronics workers in zones must endure the extremely cold air-conditioning necessary to protect the semiconductor parts. The work is primarily the bonding of microchips, which entails peering through a microscope for ten hours or more per day in order to solder gold filaments to circuit boards. This soldering process involves working with tin and lead solders that give off highly toxic fumes. The combination of severe eye-strain and daily exposure to toxic solders usually means that within less than three years' time a woman bonding microchips is no longer capable of doing the perfect work necessary for the job.

Other zone electronics workers test the completed circuits in open chemical vats of highly carcinogenic substances. Working daily in the midst of toxins like trichloroethylene, xylene, and MEX, women develop respiratory disorders, liver and kidney damage, skin rashes, and reproductive disorders. Since zone companies (and host governments) have virtually no obligations to their employees, women whose health has been affected by their employment are simply laid off, left to fend for themselves, while the continuous stream of rural poor guarantees new employees for the zones. Critics have estimated that over the past fifteen years of zone proliferation some six million Third World women below the age of thirty have been summarily "used up" and discarded by the multinational clients of the zones.[13]

Because the infrastructure is provided by the host government, foreign manufacturing companies can disappear overnight if the "favourable business climate" changes. In 1989, for instance, the subcontractor which makes clothing for "Liz Clairborne" brands (LIZ Sport, Lizwear, Play Knits) abandoned its offshore operations in the Guatemala EPZ, leaving five hundred women unpaid for their last month's work. One U.S. manager called such plants "jelly bean operations" because they can be closed down on short notice. National Semiconductor (NS) has identical offshore plants in Thailand, Indonesia, and Malaysia zones; if a political change occurs in one country the work can be immediately switched to another without interrupting the assembly cycle.

Another characteristic feature of Third World EPZs and FTZs is that there are usually very lax, or no, environmental regulations to hamper corporate industrial processes. This has been particularly appealing to the electronics industry, which (contrary to popular belief) is one of the most highly polluting industries of our time.

The process of creating silicon microchips is one that involves extensive use of fluorocarbons, gallium arsenide, freon, and trichloroethylene – all of them extremely hazardous to the environment. (Indeed, one electronics expert told me that the depletion of the ozone layer can in large part be directly attributed to the growth over the past twenty years of the electronics industry, with its massive use of fluorocarbons [CFCs] in various stages of silicon production.) To avoid both higher labour costs and more stringent environmental regulations in North America, the electronics industry has hopped from country to country, exporting its most labour-intensive and polluting processes, while head office in California's Silicon Valley dictates production quotas. Japan's electronics firms have also followed this procedure. In fact, the development of EPZs and FTZs historically parallels that industry's footloose migrations: Mexico in the early 1960s, Hong Kong in 1962, Taiwan and South Korea in the mid-1960s, Singapore in 1969, Malaysia in 1972, Thailand in 1973, Indonesia and the Philippines in 1974, Sri Lanka in 1980, African countries in the mid-1980s.

Between 1967 and 1975 foreign investment in Southeast Asia grew by 1,235 per cent – from $747 million to $9,997 million – a continuation of the Vietnam War in another guise, with primarily U.S. electronics companies reaping the benefits of cheap labour and lax environmental policy maintained in the zones. Equally significant, the microchips bonded in the zones are an integral part of the electronic weaponry – missile guidance systems, military tactical simulators, radar systems, electronics components for military aircraft, and the whole array of "smart" military technologies – developed and sold by First World countries like Canada (CEA Electronics Ltd., Canadian Marconi Co., Garrett Manufacturing Ltd., Pratt and Whitney Canada, McDonnell Douglas Canada, Litton Industries, Bombardier Inc., SNC Group Inc.) to Colombia, El Salvador, Honduras, Nigeria, Sudan, Taiwan, Thailand, Venezuela, South Korea, and Pakistan, as part of their governments' counterinsurgency and intervention programs.[14] In other words, the horribly exploited workers in such zones are, ironically enough, serving to help manufacture the very technologies used to oppress them and prevent any radical change.

What is obvious after twenty years of the Multinational Free Lunch is that EPZs and FTZs have primarily benefited the First World corporations involved and a small stratum of Third World elite. For the millions of others, the only things that have "trickled down" are greater oppression, disease, injury, pollution, and national debt. There has been no real "technology transfer" for the most part, no upgrading of skills, because the zones specialize in non-skilled and semi-skilled intermediary and labour-intensive steps in the global assembly-line. And, since working conditions are both temporary and health damaging, discarding employees after about four years in a zone plant, it is arguable that unemployment has actually increased.[15]

Nevertheless, Third World client states of the United States, Japan, Britain, and Europe are now virtually locked in to maintaining these zones, given the massive debts they incurred to establish them in the first place. Similarly, the entire Green Revolution / EPZ and FTZ phenomenon has completely altered the social structures of the countries involved: most obvious in the mass migration from rural to urban areas, but also in the formation of a new urban under-class of ex-zone workers (mostly women) whose damaged health prevents the possibility of further employment.

□

This whole sleazy set-up has depended on massive mystification in both First and Third Worlds; indeed that mystification forms a kind of "integrated circuit" of its own. Most of us North Americans have (or had) no idea that the relatively inexpensive consumer goods available on our markets are only artificially within our price range. If a just wage were paid to the millions of women who perform the labour-intensive steps in the global assembly-line, many goods — especially electronics items like microwave ovens, word processors, home computers, video games, colour TVs, VCRs — would be too expensive to market. In fact, the entire electronics industry has been built on the backs of the world's female poor.

As well, the whole story of Third World zones has had virtually no coverage in the mainstream media. As the endnotes here indicate, the relevant information has been available primarily through small leftist publications. Otherwise, for some twenty years running, our "communications revolution" of instantly up-to-date, satellite-delivered, hyper-accessible infotech news coverage has conveniently overlooked zones and the causes of Third World poverty and oppression in general.

In part this is a function of our cultural world-view: we are not meant to know the conditions of labour and production that go into the making of any of our products, since such knowledge would usually spoil our consumer pleasure. But, in a more specific sense, the overlooking of the Third World zone story is a product of the international public-relations field.

The biggest independent public-relations firms have branch-plant offices all around the world. Hill and Knowlton, for instance, maintains more than forty offices world-wide to keep abreast of international events and to serve its many governmental and corporate clients. Similarly Burson Marsteller, the second-largest independent PR firm, maintains more than two dozen offices around the world. By comparison with such extensive information networks our mainstream news organizations are minimal, maintaining only a few foreign bureaus and a few roving reporters in the news-gathering process. As a result, First World independent PR firms are often the source of "news" from remote areas of the world. As international

PR specialist Curtis Hoxtar explains, "At times we find ourselves in the position that media comes to us and says, 'Look, we'd like to know about this and this. Can you get this information for us?' And in many instances, nine out of ten cases, we get that information."[16] According to Harold Burson, "One of the big problems is that in remote parts of the world where news is happening, the cost of [media] coverage is so great these days that the number of sources from which news can be obtained is reduced materially."[17] An abiding source is the PR representative whose foreign clients pay well for favourable coverage.

There are certain instances – as in Ogilvy & Mather's PR advice to Nestlé – in which the best media-relations strategy is to "not initiate media communications" in order to "avoid generating more awareness of the issue". For twenty years this would appear to have been the case regarding Third World zones – a non-story in the mainstream press. Thus, at the same time that First World PR firms play a highly significant role in the ongoing politics of the Third World, they are also central to that "integrated circuit" of mystification by which the First World public remains ignorant of its collusion in oppressing people of the Third World.

On the other hand, Third World zone workers face a different kind of mystification. They are encouraged to think that by becoming part of the global assembly-line they will gain access to Western culture, consumer lifestyles, glamour, "progress". Instead of providing a livable wage and decent working conditions, zone companies in many countries have developed elaborate employee-relations strategies. They offer free trips to California for the most productive worker, beauty pageants and cosmetics classes for zone employees, or piped-in rock 'n roll through the sweatshops and factories. While the work is only temporary for their young female employees, the fallout in the women's lives is usually permanent.

But now, perhaps predictably enough, the entire scam has circled back on its First World origins. With business calling the shots behind the scenes as never before, potentially similar "enterprise zones" are proliferating in both Britain and the United States, with a variety of pressures in place for Canada to follow suit.

□

Over the last twenty years millions of jobs have been lost in First World countries as the footloose multinationals have shifted plants to low-wage and tax-concession havens in the Third World zones. To use the example of just one company: during the late 1970s General Electric took advantage of the abysmally low wages enforced in the zones by hiring some thirty thousand workers to do the most labour-intensive steps in the assembly of GE appliances. Meanwhile, the company laid off twenty thousand employees in the United States and fifteen thousand in Canada.[18]

The same phenomenon occurred throughout the United Kingdom in the 1970s. Though the conventional "explanation" of Britain's high rates of unemployment has been the demise of traditional manufacturing (so-called "sunset") industries – implying that Britain is simply behind the times technologically – what is left out of such an analysis is the flight of British companies to foreign zones.

For instance, the textile industry used to be one of the largest employers in Northern Ireland, but during the late 1970s companies like Courtaulds Ltd., ICI Fibres Ltd., and Du Pont Company (UK) Ltd. closed their plants and moved offshore to Third World zones. Similarly, during the 1970s more than fifty British companies set up offshore operations in the Philippines alone, where eleven EPZs courted multinational clients by providing the basic zone Free Lunch.[19]

EPZs and FTZs make it possible for corporations to seek out the least stringent environmental regulations, the most generous tax concessions, and the cheapest non-unionized labour forces anywhere in the world (usually hired to work for less than fifty U.S. cents per hour). One result is that, around the world, worker is pitted against worker as jobs are lost in one country by being shifted to another with a more "favourable business environment". Another result is that unions are increasingly hamstrung, not only by repressive zone policy but by the new economic structure itself. As one organizer puts it, "How do you strike a multinational?" – when it can simply shift operations to another zone or another country virtually overnight. The best recent example in Canada is that of Fleck Manufacturing, which in autumn 1988, in the midst of a strike, simply emptied its Ontario shop over a weekend and fled to Mexico.

The latest irony, however, is that both Britain and the United States have recently implemented the "enterprise zone" idea in their own countries as a "solution" to the unemployment and economic blight caused by their globe-hopping multinationals in the first place. As Wendy McKeen, researcher for the Women's Bureau of the Canadian Labour Congress, wrote in her 1984 study of zones:

The argument is that unless special benefits are provided and concessions made to industry in industrialized countries, there is nothing to stop it from continuing to relocate and expand into developing countries where those benefits and concessions are to be found. The national governments of Britain and the U.S. have reasoned that they have to do something to keep industry in their own countries and that "something" is the enterprise zone.[20]

What is also clear is that both the Thatcher and Reagan-Bush governments have desired to loose the so-called fetters imposed on free enterprise at home. As Reagan put it in his 1983 endorsement of the federal enterprise zone concept, "The Enterprise Zone approach would remove government barriers, freeing individuals to create, produce and earn their own wages and profits."[21] Margaret "There is no alternative" Thatcher calls this "people's capitalism", a bit of PR rhetoric that has gotten a fair amount of play in the press. Arguably, however, the enterprise zone concept is part of the drive to overturn all gains made by the labour movement during the postwar years. It is also a frontal attack on the environment, since enterprise zones and the highly polluting electronics industries go hand-in-hand. As we approach the millennium, the neo-conservative desire, evident in the Mulroney government as well, is nothing less than a return to capitalism-in-the-raw. Finding euphemisms for that desire has been a significant challenge to governmental and private-sector "communications" specialists.

□

The idea of enterprise zones in Britain originated with city planner Peter Hall, a Reading University professor, who in 1977 proposed that "small, selected areas of inner cities ... be simply thrown open to all kinds of initiative with minimum control. In other words, we would aim to recreate the Hong Kong of the 1950s and 1960s inside Liverpool or inner Glasgow."[22] Hall's chosen analogy of Hong Kong was by no means gratuitous, since his plan was specifically geared towards attracting high-tech expertise – the most footloose fraternity within an extremely footloose industry. As Hall wrote:

> The only way we are going to tempt it [science-based industry] back into the cities, if at all, is through a very imaginative program that deliberately caters for the whims of such people. That means the

creation of high-amenity environments ... plus adjacent high income housing schemes, plus motorways for them to drive their cars from the outer suburbs.[23]

In addition to enterprise zones geared to meet the "whims" of microelectronics expertise, Hall proposed that more freeports be added in Britain, admitting that such areas are "based on fairly shameless free enterprise". Free of corporate taxes, social services, industrial and environmental regulations, customs barriers and tar-iffs, freeports also ban the closed shop and legislated minimum wages; wages are left (in Hall's words) "to reach their own level by the normal processes of bargaining".[24]

Hall's ideas appealed to the Conservative Party's economics spokesperson, Sir Geoffrey Howe, who was interested in attracting business investment into the densely populated cores of Britain's urban ghettoes. The election of Margaret Thatcher in 1979 resulted in Howe's becoming Chancellor of the Exchequer (Secretary of the Treasury), a post that allowed him to make the idea of enterprise zones a top government priority. In Howe's view, "Impediments to job creation, such as the closed shop and the minimum wage laws, would not operate in the zones."[25]

The Thatcher government initiated zone legislation in 1979. While more moderate than either Hall's proposals or Howe's, the legislation nonetheless granted generous concessions to zone businesses, including exemption from industrial and commercial property taxes, income tax concessions, customs relaxation, tax hol-idays on construction, and speedy disposal of bureaucratic red tape. The legislation dovetailed nicely with other governmental moves towards privatization and deregulation. In 1979 Thatcher began turning over a significant number of nationalized industries to pri-vate companies, abolishing wage and price controls, selling off government-owned land and housing, and examining ways to reduce the impact of rent control throughout the country – including elim-inating it for zone areas.

When the enterprise zone legislation was discussed in the British parliament, it evoked heated opposition from the Labour Party, which called it "swashbuckling capitalism". Nevertheless, the legis-lation was passed in 1980. Economist Stuart Butler, policy analyst for the ultra-conservative think-tank The Heritage Foundation in the United States, found some irony in the situation:

Despite the bitter denunciations by the NEC [National Executive Council of the Labour Party] and the Labour MPs, Labour-controlled local councils almost fell over themselves to submit applications for sites – much to the chagrin of the NEC and the amusement of Conservatives. Almost all the applicants, and the cities finally chosen, have Labour councils.[26]

Between June 1981 and April 1982 eleven sites were designated as enterprise zones, most averaging 500 acres: eight in England, at Corby, Dudley, Hartlepool, the Isle of Dogs, Newcastle upon Tyne, Salford / Trafford, Speke (Liverpool) and Wakefield; one in the Lower Swansea Valley in Wales; one at Clydebank near Glasgow in Scotland; and one in Belfast, Northern Ireland. At each site the government invested in infrastructure and reclamation programs to create those "high-amenity environments" suited to the "whims" of electronics experts, while environment minister Michael Heseltine launched programs to attract industry to the zones, using the generous tax concessions as the primary incentive.

□

Although the public-relations rhetoric behind enterprise zones is that they are not intended to attract multinational clients but instead are meant to foster "small businesses", in practice it has not always worked out that way. The Scottish Development Agency heavily promoted its zone under the rubric of "Silicon Glen", thereby attracting megacorporations like IBM, Nippon Electric Company (NEC), Hewlett-Packard, Wang, Motorola, and National Semiconductor (NS). By 1982, 40 per cent of the microchips made in Western Europe were being manufactured in Scotland, with the multinationals gobbling up the tax concessions to employ some 34,000 people. Similarly, Wales attracted Mitel Corporation of Canada (later bought up by British Telecom) for the manufacture of electronic switchboards, integrated circuits, and hybrid circuits; U.S. Corning Glass for a fibre optics plant; Inmost Corporation for the building of a microchip plant; and offshore operations run by Sony, Aiwa, and Seikisui.[27]

By 1984 Thatcher decided to cut regional spending. As reported in The Globe and Mail, "The Government no longer aims at the regeneration of hard-hit regions. If depressed areas are to pick up economically, it will be only as a consequence of a recovery in the economy generally; no particular measures will be taken to help whole regions."[28] Apparently, regional development policy was subsumed by enterprise zone policy, since the decision coincided with the creation of fourteen more enterprise zones: in Glandford (Humberside), Middlesbrough, northeast Lancashire, northwest Kent, Rotherham, Sunthrope, Telford, Wellingborough and Workington (now Allerdale) in England; at Delyn and Milford Haven Waterway in Wales; at Invergordon and Tayside in Scotland; and in Londonderry, Northern Ireland.

The government's claims in the mid-1980s that its enterprise zone policy had created forty-eight thousand jobs were somewhat misleading. In Wales, for instance, unemployment remained at 17 per cent in 1985, suggesting that megacorporation investment was primarily managerial for tax purposes. Some critics have claimed that Britain's enterprise zones are essentially "yuppie havens" that "revitalize" certain areas and relocate the already employed while driving low-income and unemployed people out of the areas. Although newspapers have often been filled with paeans to Thatcher's "economic miracle", it is not entirely clear just what that "miracle" entails. So far, British companies operating in foreign EPZs and FTZs do not appear to have been lured back home, nor is there any guarantee that the multinationals which have set up in some of the enterprise zones will stay there once the ten-year Free Lunch runs out. In the summer of 1989, for example, Wang pulled out of Silicon Glen and moved elsewhere, having received more than $1 million from the British government during its brief stay.

The real effect of Thatcher's economic policy is to have crippled the unions and increased the inequities between rich and poor. While two million Britons remain unemployed, the average British worker still hands over a third of his or her pay in taxes. As Edward Greenspon wrote in *The Globe and Mail* (May 2, 1989), "The gains of the rich outstrip those of average workers by two to one and those without work have actually fallen back. One in eight Britons lives below the poverty line, according to the European Commission. 'The economy has been divided into those who have jobs and those who don't have jobs,' said Labour Party advisor Meghned Desai, an economist at the London School of Economics. 'Those are the haves and the have nots.'"[29]

Moreover, the decision to court high-tech industries does not bode well for several reasons, including the staunchly anti-union policy of virtually all electronics corporations, their hideous irresponsibility towards the environment, and (most ironic) the goal of high tech itself, "jobless growth". In this sense, the British White Paper of January 1988 is a sign of the times.

□

Third World EPZs and FTZs have primarily benefited First World electronics companies, whose phenomenal growth over the last twenty years has in turn led to increased automation at all work-sites (factory, office, even farm). In the United Kingdom one million manufacturing jobs were lost in the period 1980-82 alone, in part because of offshore moves and the global recession, but also as a result of increased factory automation. Similarly, automation helped U.S. Steel, for example, to reduce its U.S. workforce from 28,000 in 1979 to less than 9,000 in 1986. Automakers in Detroit plan to install an additional 25,000 robots by the early 1990s, displacing between 75,000 and 100,000 human workers.[30]

For all their rhetoric about "jobs, jobs, jobs", First World governments are fully committed to the high-tech agenda of (to use the jargon) "labour-shedding" to eliminate this unfortunate drain on profits. The British White Paper of January 1988 spells out an economic policy for the future based on rapid advances in all high-tech fields, especially "biotechnology and advanced integrated manufacturing systems". As the Paper explains, Britain's Department of Trade and Industry (DTI), the department responsible for the new "enterprise culture", is expected to facilitate business by "currently running collaborative programmes in advanced robotics and gallium arsenide (a semiconductor material with the potential to provide very fast microelectronic operations) and a new programme on superconductivity is now being launched."[31]

The goal of biotechnology is the development of the biochip, smaller than a grain of sand, to be implanted into living species, as well as gene-splicing and genetic engineering for multiple uses of increased "efficiency". As Jeremy Rifkin writes in *Algeny*, his book about biotechnology:

> The grand objective is to turn living material into biocomputers and then to use these biocomputers to further engineer living materials. In the future, biocomputers will be engineered directly into living systems, just as microcomputers are engineered into mechanical systems

today. They will monitor activity, adjust performance, speed up and slow down metabolic activity, transform living material into products, and perform a host of other supervisory functions.[32]

Dozens of multinationals have jumped on the biotech bandwagon, including Du Pont, General Electric, Upjohn, Exxon, Allied Corporation, Phillips Petroleum, Kodak, Dow, and most of the giant Japanese corporations. Behind closed doors they have lobbied effectively to convince First World governments, already technophile in orientation, that biotechnology is the next "necessary" step in economic and technological "progress". This high-tech revolution on all fronts is nothing less than what could be called "downloading the planet" – transforming species into more perfect and efficient simulacra – while unchecked environmental pillage eliminates the rest. Nonetheless, in terms of achieving social consensus on this issue, multinationals have been virtually unchallenged. Indeed, it is a given in our culture that technological development must proceed unimpeded.

To prepare the younger generations for their roles as superfluous machine-tenders, fast-food hamburger helpers, and a very tiny elite of high-tech wizards, the British White Paper states that "The DTI will publicise a range of possible activities to bring schools and businesses together, particularly through employer involvement in curriculum development, school and college management, and enterprise activities in schools". Educational training is to be "targeted on the needs of local employers".[33] Thus corporate industry is to be allowed an even greater public-relations role in childhood education – a development that is occurring on this side of the Atlantic as well.[34]

Britain's "enterprise culture" – for which the enterprise zones are supposedly the centrepiece – is based on the most hideously narrow vision of human beings, and of the future, possible. Nevertheless, the Iron Maiden has inspired the United States to take "enterprise culture" even further.

In the United States the ultra-conservative Heritage Foundation has played a dominant public-relations role in promoting the enterprise zone concept throughout the 1980s. As a think-tank, it has generated an extraordinary mass of PR material, including frequent press releases on every Congressional development regarding the issue, promotional press kits, and, of course, public-affairs lobbying behind the scenes. The respected voice of neo-conservative thought, the Heritage Foundation has been influential on many fronts throughout the decade; but on the issue of enterprise zones it has been the work of Foundation policy analyst and economist Stuart Butler that is credited with first transporting the concept from Britain to the United States and then lobbying persuasively at the highest levels to achieve endorsement and action.

Butler has been unflinching with regard to the central thrust that will make the U.S. enterprise zones more successful than Britain's so far: suspension or "relaxation" of minimum wage laws. He argues that minimum wage laws only create unemployment by pricing the young and unskilled out of the labour market; and that their suspension within an enterprise zone will provide "new opportunities" for all those masses of unemployed in the "depressed central cities". If minimum wages can't be relaxed, another option Butler recommends is "some kind of subsidy or tax credit for those hiring labor in the zones".[35] Butler has also posed the idea of a "youth minimum wage – lower than the standard minimum" for the U.S. federal zones.

Arguably, such thinking harks back to the days of nineteenth-century tycoons like John D. Rockefeller, who believed that wages were a charity bestowed by business on undeserving labour; thus the seeming beneficence of business – demonstrated simply by bothering to hire anybody at all in these days of automation and Third World low-wage havens – is to be rewarded not only by generous tax concessions but also by dropping minimum wages and / or giving tax credits to those who hire in the U.S. zones.

Not surprisingly, the enterprise zone concept was immediately embraced by Republican Congressman Jack Kemp, appointed Secretary for Housing and Urban Development (HUD) under Bush. Kemp has been pumping for federal enterprise zone legislation since 1979. His recurring PR pitch is based on the felicitous phrase, "greenlining American cities", which invites the question of just whose pockets are to be lined with green. The original Kemp-Garcia bill, tabled in Congress in 1979, proposed generous and highly controversial tax incentives for the zones, including a special investment tax credit (of 3 to 10 per cent) for capital investment (in addition to the existing investment tax credit); exemption from capital gains tax; business losses to be carried against tax for up to twenty years; a 10 per cent employer tax credit and a 5 per cent employee tax credit on salaries paid for work inside a federal enterprise zone; a tax credit of 50 per cent of the wages paid to poor workers and those from disadvantaged groups for the first three years of employment, declining by 10 percentage points a year thereafter; industrial development bonds to finance businesses in a zone; state and local tax relief; and ease of planning regulations and controls at the federal, state, and local levels.[36]

In his 1983 State of the Union message Reagan announced that his administration was fully behind such federal enterprise zones, but the legislation remained blocked in the House Ways and Means Committee. Meanwhile, thirty-three states moved to enact their own legislation for "state enterprise zones". Connecticut led the way with its bold program to abolish property taxes in a zone for five years, to provide exemption from state sales tax and a 50 per cent cut in state corporate income tax, to establish a tax credit of $1,000 for each full-time job created in a zone, and to provide access to low-cost start-up and expansion loans.[37] Similar forms of corporate Free Lunch were enacted in thirty other states throughout the 1980s.

Minimum wage legislation is a state concern: there are nine states that have no minimum wage and twelve with a minimum wage below $3.00 per hour. Similarly, there are twenty "right to work" states, with low unionization and inferior employment standards regarding anti-discrimination laws, equal pay for women, or overtime pay. These features also became part of the "favourable business climate" hyped in state enterprise zone PR efforts, coinciding with the fact that during the Reagan years union membership fell to less than 17 per cent of the nation's labour – the lowest percentage in the industrialized world.[38]

The subsequent self-promotion and PR hustling on the part of state enterprise zone boosters have yielded a variety of Silicon Valley clones, at least as presented by press-kit hype: Silicon Prairie (Texas), Silicon Mountain (Colorado), Silicon Desert (Arizona), Silicon Bayou (Louisiana), Silicon Tundra (Minnesota), Silicon Forest (Oregon), Silicon Valley East (Troy-Albany-Schenectady, New York). It's clear what kind of job creation is desired. It's also clear that "enterprise culture" does not necessarily foster the imagination.

On February 4, 1988, legislation was enacted at the federal level (Bill #HR 7) allowing HUD to designate one hundred federal enterprise zones eligible for federal tax monies to aid infrastructure development. Nevertheless in most circles the legislation has been seen as a largely "symbolic" provision since it lacks the necessary federal tax concessions that would make the zones attractive to business. As Mike Savage of HUD told me, "The current legislation is an empty bucket since it is without tax incentives. The problem is that only the federal government can rebate federal taxes." His HUD colleague Stephen Glaude adds, "We're hoping for a federal bill that would provide tax incentives and regulatory relief. Regulations that protect people should stay, like handling toxic wastes, but this has been an age of over-regulation, much of which is more interference than protection."[39]

Consequently HUD secretary Kemp in the spring of 1989 ordered a delay on the designation of federal enterprise zone sites until different legislation is passed. The preferred legislation was succinctly outlined by Heritage Foundation's Stuart Butler in a press release of March 31, 1989, calling for "an entrepreneurial climate" in the zones by providing "employment tax credits to reduce the cost of labour" and "incentives to investors and lenders" including "full relief from capital gains tax, or a limited tax deduction" for investors.[40]

There are currently six bills before Congress concerning federal enterprise zones, and ongoing field hearings on the issue have commenced. The political climate surrounding federal tax relief in the zones is favourable. According to HUD's Mike Savage, "President Bush is prepared for $1 billion of lost tax revenues associated with enterprise zones." U.S. corporations already successfully dodge more than $21 billion in taxes every year through loopholes. The pending zone legislation will likely further legitimize and increase the Free Lunch through employment tax credits and relief from federal capital gains tax. The lost revenues will, of course, be made up by further shifting of the tax burden. As HUD's Stephen Glaude explains, the federal enterprise zones "will yield tax revenues because of the jobs". In other words, employees will be taxed more than enough to make up for the concessions to business. Evidently, Bush's "kinder, gentler America" means more coddling for you-know-who.

Meanwhile HUD continues to receive requests for federal enterprise zone status from around the country. The footloose U.S. multinationals appear to have left behind them a wake of impoverishment and grief over the past twenty years. As Savage puts it, "We've received 270 applications for designation, including from places like Watts, the South Bronx, Harlem, Louisville, Kentucky. But there are at least a thousand areas whose 'distress criteria' would make them eligible."

☐

The ultra-conservative Fraser Institute in British Columbia has been promoting the idea of free trade zones within Canada throughout the 1980s. Its scenario for FTZs here includes suspension of minimum wage legislation; the waiving of compulsory employer and employee contributions to unemployment insurance, the Canada Pension Plan, and public medical insurance; the prohibition of closed shops "and other restrictive practices of unions". The Fraser Institute has urged an alliance of business firms and regional development agencies to lobby for FTZs.[41]

In 1984 the B.C. government announced that it "has been actively pursuing the prospect of establishing one or more 'duty free zones' in our Province.... Duty free zones would increase trade flows and foreign investment." According to Wendy McKeen's research, a variety of city governments have also expressed interest in establishing FTZs within their cities, including Montreal, Halifax, Hamilton, Winnipeg, Edmonton, and Port St. John.[42]

During the mid-1980s two provinces established zones of sorts and have attempted to promote them. Newfoundland's International Trade Zone at Stephenville utilizes a former military base that includes buildings, a runway, and a harbour, with a variety of customs programs available, as well as low-rent occupancy of infrastructure for businesses. For four years Nova Scotia's Sydport International Trade Zone on Cape Breton Island promoted its 600 acres of land, partially serviced with utilities and factory buildings, and its "large pool of willing skilled workers to draw from". But on February 28, 1989, Sydport was closed down permanently.

Industry Trade and Technology Minister Donald Cameron blamed Ottawa for Sydport's demise, stating in his press release: "The board of directors of SITZ has been trying over a period of four years to convince the federal government of the benefits of free trade zones and to make necessary changes in federal legislation to permit their operation."[43] Mr. Cameron's office did not return my phone calls, so it is not clear what those "necessary changes in federal legislation" entailed. Presumably they would have had to do with federal tax concessions, altered labour legislation, and relaxation of customs tariffs and duties.

While the closing of Sydport might suggest that the Mulroney government does not embrace the principles and practices at work in free trade zones, the wider economic context — especially the free trade deal — indicates a more disturbing process underway. In 1984, Wendy McKeen's research paper noted: "Canada has very recently moved closer to adopting the free enterprise zone concept. The federal government is currently being pressured to keep up with the times by applying the zone idea here." Citing the federal Throne Speech of 1983, in which the government announced an export-oriented economic policy under which " 'duty free export zones' will be established for the manufacturing and processing in bond of goods for export", McKeen states, on the basis of extensive interviews:

> Since the December 1983 Throne Speech senior bureaucrats in several government departments have been working on what "duty free zones" will mean for Canada. They are considering questions like the following. Would free trade zones benefit Canada? How could they be made attractive enough to business? What function would they serve? What impact would they have on employment? What would or should a Canadian free trade zone look like?[44]

In answer to these questions, especially the last one, we might consider the case of Mexico, which provides some timely lessons for Canadians.

In 1965 the Mexican Secretary of Industry and Commerce was taken by U.S. industrialists on a tour to Hong Kong and Taiwan, where he observed the extensive U.S. assembly-plants being set up in the Southeast Asian free trade zones. Convinced (wrongly, as it turned out) that an FTZ would bring "technology transfer" and a solution to massive unemployment (caused in part by the "Green Revolution" pitched to Mexico in the 1950s), government officials signed the Border Industrialization Program (BIP). The BIP created an FTZ out of a twelve-and-a-half-mile stretch along the Mexico-U.S. border. Based on a "maquiladora" system of "twinned" production plants on both sides of the border, the Mexican plants have provided cheap, non-unionized labour for unskilled and semi-skilled assembly work, while the U.S. plants (located in low- or no-minimum-

wage states of the Sunbelt) have co-ordinated production and provided the finishing steps for products.[45]

By 1972 this program was expanded to make the entire country of
Mexico a free trade zone, with a current minimum wage of $3.20
U.S. per day. More than twelve hundred U.S. firms have set up
assembly-plants inside Mexico, employing nearly one million workers (mostly women) in plants similar to FTZ plants elsewhere: with
minimal health and safety standards, high quotas, high stress, no job
security or benefits, and abysmally low wages.[46]

Mexico was the first instance in which *an entire country* was
declared a free trade zone, thereby removing all barriers to the
"favourable business climate" desired by globe-hopping multinationals. It is plausible that Canada's free trade agreement accom-
plishes much the same thing – though the PR rhetoric favouring the
deal could never mention such a goal. If, as McKeen tells us, federal
bureaucrats have been considering questions of "what a Canadian
free trade zone would look like" since the early 1980s, the answer is
probably this: it would look like what the country is set to become
under the free trade deal. This would not necessarily mean a proliferation of enclosed zone-sites of several hundred acres, but rather an
opening up of the entire country to the philosophy and practices at
work in free trade zones. Given Canada's unique situation as a country that has First World development and, in many ways, Third
World status (through a foreign-owned economy), the long-term
repercussions of the free trade deal will likely manifest both sides of
the FTZ coin.

On the one hand, as critics of the deal have recognized, it disman-
tles crucial customs protections and tariffs, opens the way for even
greater resource-extraction by U.S. firms, hands over 299 service
industries to U.S. management, threatens our more stringent environmental protection and health and safety standards through "har-
monizing" with those of the United States, gives "national treatment" to U.S. corporations located below the border, threatens
regional development policy and social programs as "unfair subsidies", and further opens the door to multinational desires.

On the other hand, the free trade deal forces Canadian-owned
companies to compete on a world market dominated by "the global
assembly-line". In other words, to survive, Canadian firms must
imitate the behaviour and practices of multinationals. Rather than
serve our own local, regional, and national markets and needs,

Canadian companies must now jump on the bandwagon of export-oriented production. As the Throne Speech of April 4, 1989, declared: "My government is providing programs to assist small and medium-sized business to develop export opportunities that are emerging as a result of the free trade agreement.... The federal government is also placing greater emphasis on the Asia-Pacific region as well as on Europe."[47]

Translated, this likely means greater Canadian corporate involvement in offshore operations in Southeast Asian EPZs and FTZs in order to cut costs and compete for new international markets, including the Single European Market set to be established in 1992 and the new China opening up to foreign investment and a rash of consumer goods.

Playing follow-the-leader to Thatcher and Reagan-Bush, the Mulroney government has embraced privatization, with the Throne Speech promising "further privatization of those crown corporations which no longer serve a public policy role" and "passage of business framework legislation which will contribute to the smooth functioning of a modern economy". In all three countries the neo-conservative agenda is that government facilitate business by cutting back on the government's intervening role in the economy. Already the Mulroney government (following the advice of the BCNI) has "restructured" the unemployment insurance program, axed $4 billion from public day care, and cut funding to health and education. The Wilson budget of 1989 was a blatant concession to big business, further shifting the tax burden to working people through a new national sales tax that will tax virtually every item and service except food.

Arguably, this manoeuvre is in keeping with the philosophy behind enterprise zones. As Stuart Butler has explained in the United States, tax concessions to business are to be made up by new taxes on employees. Thus the idea that Canada has in effect become a country-wide FTZ is further borne out by the 1989 budget's generosity to corporations, part of creating a "favourable business climate" necessary for any free trade zone.

The 1989 Throne Speech also announced the Mulroney government's full commitment to "biotechnology, advanced industrial materials, and information technology" – the high-tech agenda being pushed by the most powerful multinationals. While Canada's rivers and lakes are dying, its forests decimated, its topsoil blowing away, and many of its people are facing increasing impoverishment, our government has revealed its high-tech priorities by jumping on a bandwagon that is geared not only to "jobless growth" but also to rampant pollution and a surfeit of even more unnecessary consumer gadgets. Just at a time when we could, and should, be moving towards an economy based on sovereignty to ensure environmental protection, massive recycling programs, limits to needless production and consumerism, and the necessities of social justice (including justice towards the Third World), Mulroney and his cronies have been sucked into the very same multinational public-relations scam pitched to U.S. client-states in the Third World back in the early 1960s: an export-oriented economy to replace import-substitution plans, land reform, and national sovereignty itself.

The irony is that, for all its seemingly futuristic orientation (enhanced by sexy high-tech talk), the current agenda of Canada, Britain, and the United States is the most backward-looking vision possible. What it looks back to is mid-nineteenth-century capitalism-in-the-raw, complete with extremes of rich and poor, intolerable pollution, and non-unionization – an apt description of everybody's current role-model, Silicon Valley in California.[48] As the Multinational Free Lunch takes in more and more of the world – through export processing zones, free trade zones, enterprise zones, and free trade deals – the business / government collusion is fast eating up any semblance of social justice that may once have tempered the ravages of so-called free enterprise. Nevertheless, the expanding role of public-relations practice will no doubt ensure that the neo-conservative agenda unfolds smoothly. Unfortunately the whole set-up makes even liberalism look good.

6

The "Greening" of
Establishment PR:
Mind Pollution on the Rise

It is a happy coincidence that just when it is becoming clear
that some technologies are seriously threatening the environment, the recently developed peaceful use of atomic energy is
available to mitigate the threat.

D.S. LAWSON, President of AECL's CANDU reactor operations

ON THE COVER OF *The National Geographic* for December 1988
there is a double-hologram depicting planet Earth. Beneath the
image are the words, "As we begin our second century, the Geographic asks: Can Man Save This Fragile Earth?" Viewed from one
angle, the holographic image shows the planet round and whole,
with its North Pole tilted slightly down and towards the left, showing the North American continent, the U.S.S.R., Europe, and Scandi-
navia. Viewed from a different angle, the holographic image shows
planet Earth breaking apart, with pieces flying off it like chunks of
broken glass. Conceived as an "action hologram", it is a fascinating
cover, suitable for an issue devoted (almost) entirely to "fragile
Earth".

The back cover of the issue is also a double-hologram made with
the same special technology developed to create the front cover. The
back cover depicts a McDonald's restaurant with a golden arches
sign that reads "Over 10,000 Opened". Viewed from one angle, the
restaurant is bathed in sunshine to depict daytime. Inside the building little human figures can be seen lined up at the counter. Viewed
from a different angle, the restaurant (which, unlike the front-cover
planet, does not change position) is seen at night. The sunlight has
disappeared, but inside the building the lights are on and the little
human figures are still lined up at the counter. The "action" in this

double-hologram is the change from day to night, from an exterior light source to an interior one. Underneath the image is a prominent quotation: "None Of Us Is As Good As All Of Us". Smaller ad-copy beneath the quotation explains, "Whether applied to the issues of a growing business or a growing world, the words of McDonald's founder Ray Kroc are equally relevant."

The front and back covers of this issue of *The National Geographic* must be seen as a dialogue, a subtle communication from cover to cover, front to back, hologram to hologram, rather than as happenstance or accidental. Although the magazine's editorial office has assured me that McDonald's did not pay for the front cover hologram, nonetheless the company's use of the same technology to create its back-cover institutional ad indicates that the presentation must be seen as a corporate response to the front cover's double-hologram. Conceived as the reassuring counterpart to the disturbing image and question presented on the front of the magazine, and appearing as the "last word" in an issue devoted to environmental pillage, the McDonald's institutional hologram reveals the stunning finesse with which corporate public relations now operates.

One of the primary dictates of contemporary PR is that "A corporation must sell itself as well as its product".[1] In this instance McDonald's has pitched itself as an institution that is more stable than the planet itself. The corporate hubris involved in this back cover is a subtle, multi-levelled effort that, coming from a major polluter, is breathtaking.

What is immediately noticeable is that there is no angle from which the McDonald's restaurant can be seen to be breaking apart, with pieces flying off it, like planet Earth on the front cover. Apparently, although the Earth is endangered McDonald's is not. The supposed stability of the institution is reinforced by the fact that the depicted restaurant does not change position, as the Earth does on the front cover. As well, the "action" in the two covers is decidedly different in tone. On the front, the change in viewing angle yields a shock, a startling sight of the planet breaking apart. On the back cover, however, there is only a pleasurable surprise: the change of angle shows the passage of time from day to night, a familiar change that contributes to the aura of stability and reassurance being created around the corporate institution.

Unlike the front of the magazine, the captioning text on the back raises no questions; instead it subtly provides the answer to that anxious question posed on the front: "Can Man Save This Fragile Earth?" The response comes from McDonald's founder Ray Kroc and his immortalized words: "None Of Us Is As Good As All Of Us". The intentional ambiguity of these words makes them a kind of corporate "koan" posed by the pseudo-Zen-master of multinational business. At first glance the quotation seems an affirmation of global solidarity, a commitment to the good of all people, beyond individualistic or corporate gain. Based on our propensity to skim ads, this first level of meaning carries a resonance of corporate responsibility. As well, the Kroc quotation may seem a rallying cry to stir us all into environmental action, since obviously "none of us is as good as all of us" when it comes to trying to save the endangered planet.

But this first impression of founder Kroc's words must be tempered, since the quotation is followed by smaller ad-copy that clarifies his tantalizing "koan". We are told that the founder's words are relevant "whether applied to the issues of a growing business or a growing world". This sounds much more like business-as-usual, rather than the altruistic solidarity first conveyed by Kroc's saying. We begin to perceive that the "all of us" mentioned in his quotation has nothing to do with the general public at all; instead it is a reference to another piece of information in the institutional hologram: the golden-arches sign reading "Over 10,000 Opened." With McDonald's growth as a corporate cloner over the past thirty years, certainly one McDonald's could never be as good as all of them, according to the bottom line.

In this sense, a different Kroc quote would have been less ambiguous. "This is rat eat rat, dog eat dog," said founder Ray in the early years with regard to competitors. "I'm going to kill 'em before they kill me. You're talking about the American way of survival of the fittest."[2] But of course this would not be the kind of communications message the McDonald's PR team has in mind, especially in the context of "fragile Earth". Rather, the founder's ambiguous statement and the explanatory text accompanying it subtly pose an alternative re-naming or re-captioning of that disturbing double-hologram on the front cover. Instead of thinking of the planet as breaking apart under environmental stress and throwing off broken bits, we might consider it "a growing world" figuratively bursting at the seams with expansionary business, growing as fast as McDonald's with its more than ten thousand restaurants opened world-wide.

But Kroc's words, we are told, are also relevant to any "growing business". In this sense, "None Of Us Is As Good As All Of Us" may be read as a rallying cry to the corporate sector, though just what they are to rally around is, again, intentionally obscure. The meaning comes from the magazine itself, which after all is the context for the back-cover ad.

The articles included in this issue of *The National Geographic* implicate many aspects of a Western lifestyle (both corporate and personal) based on planetary exploitation and environmental irresponsibility. In particular, "Population, Plenty, and Poverty", a lengthy article by ecologists Paul Ehrlich and Anne Ehrlich, makes vivid cross-cultural comparisons of the ways of living in six different countries. The section dealing with the United States is headed "Geared to Consumption" and reveals that per capita energy consumption in the country is forty times greater than in four of the other nations examined, Kenya, China, India, and Brazil, and more than twice as great as in the fifth country, Hungary. The U.S. section of the article even includes a full-page colour photograph of an American family seated in their car, gorging on McDonald's junk food. The corporate logo is clearly visible on the packaging for the french fries and soft drinks. It is precisely here that we can see the supreme corporate confidence and finesse at work in the back-cover ad.

McDonald's can tolerate an inside photograph that implicates it, in part because the company will have the last word, providing closure to our experience of the magazine and its two hundred pages of environmental information. That closure is an important aspect of "issues management", including the corporate "largesse" in helping to sponsor this particular issue of *The National Geographic*. A back-cover ad in the magazine costs far more than the $121,000 price-tag for a one-page ad inside. And in this instance the holographic parallels from cover to cover imply McDonald's born-again environmentalism, at least at first glance.

Since one of the primary issues now confronting all corporate activity is the politics of the environment, the McDonald's holographic institutional ad might be seen as a kind of instructional primer, provided by founder Ray Kroc and his PR team to other "growing businesses", on just how to engage with the current challenge to business-as-usual.

The back cover neatly meets the challenge by showing us the

McDonald's "world", an alternative to the front-cover depiction since it is stable, unthreatening, familiar, reassuring, unchanging. The institution has been around long enough to have become (or assume itself to be) a symbol of stability: serving us, reassuring us, providing a clean, well-lighted place where (as the hologram depicts) nothing more startling occurs than a change from day to night. It is a "world" that seems to exist entirely for our benefit, our pleasure. "You deserve a break today," the electronic ads have told us.

By contrast, the breaking-world depicted on the front cover is threatening, unfamiliar, demanding. Indeed this disturbing image, as well as much of the information between the two covers, asks for nothing less than a radical change of lifestyle, a paradigm-shift in both consciousness and consumer behaviour, if fragile Earth is to continue existing beyond its currently doomed prognosis. But McDonald's knows that our present concern is not yet enough to change our ways. In fact the evidence is there in its hologram, in the sign claiming "Over 10,000 Opened". We may read this issue of *The National Geographic* and contemplate the implications of the information therein, but it does not really penetrate to the core where real change occurs and then leads to profoundly different ways of living. It is in this sense that the corporate institution is unthreatened, can even play on our anxieties about "fragile Earth" and co-opt those concerns for its own purposes. Perhaps even more important, whatever we may know about McDonald's own thirty-year-long contribution to the depletion of the ozone layer, the elimination of the rain forests, and the mounting garbage problem, the corporation can point to us: for, after all, "We do it all for you".

Thus, at this point in time, the only real threats to the "growing business" advocated in the ad are the so-called extremist environmentalists and the possibility of more stringent regulatory measures world-wide. And here we begin to grasp the deepest level of Ray Kroc's "koan". It is a subtle rallying cry to other corporate public-relations practitioners, especially public-affairs specialists; for, when it comes to both issues management and preventing protectionist environmental regulation and legislation, "None Of Us Is As Good As All Of Us".

□

The escalating environmental crisis has knocked a huge "legitimacy gap" into the North American way of "life". This is a lifestyle addicted to fossil fuels and geared to an economy based on built-in obsolescence, disposable products, unlimited consumption, and a concept of "progress" that means defining the planet primarily as "natural resources" for human exploitation. It is becoming obvious that this way of life is no longer viable. Each crisis highlights the polarization taking place between radical and reformist environmental perspectives.

For example, the Exxon Valdez oil spill off the Alaskan coast in March 1989 resulted in a consumer boycott in which thousands cut up their credit cards and mailed them to Exxon's arrogant CEO, Lawrence G. Rawl – who not only claimed the catastrophe was an "act of God" but also compared it favourably to Union Carbide's Bhopal disaster because Exxon had "nobody dead".[3] The consumer boycott, as well as much of the media commentary accompanying the spill, avoided the larger issue at stake. Not only were there thirteen other oil spills in the three months preceding Valdez, but the whole notion of "reforming" the oil industry's practices was also considered by many to be a cop-out. An editorial in Pollution Probe's *Probe Post* stated:

> So what, then, is the answer to the question of how to stop such spills from happening, a question which so many people have debated in the media following the spills? Well, for those who rank the environment as one of their greatest concerns, the answer has nothing to do with creating new cleanup technology, nothing to do with testing ship captains for drugs or alcohol and nothing to do with oil-spill preparedness on the part of the army, coast guard, etc. The answer is simple: leave oil in the ground and take immediate and firm action to promote energy conservation and development of alternative energy sources. Environmentalists have been pointing out the hows and whys of such a shift in energy policy for years.[4]

The idea of "leaving oil in the ground" (and trees in the forest, minerals in the mountains, fish in the sea) has now become the crucial dividing line separating political perspectives. Since environmental concern is no longer a "lunatic fringe" issue (as it was once characterized), it has become a litmus test indicating the degree to which individuals and organizations, as well as politicians and corporations, have a stake in maintaining the status quo. Obviously, widespread radical change in the way we live our daily lives is a threat to both a power structure and an economy that need us to be diligent consumers. As a result, the "greening" of corporate and governmental personas is rapidly becoming the standard PR strategy in order to hold out the promise of "reform" and prevent radical change.

This is in itself a sign that more than twenty-five years of environmental action (dating from the 1962 publication of Rachel Carson's book *Silent Spring*) is bearing fruit in terms of public consciousness. A recent *Financial Post* article by Stephen Duncan, former Shell Canada PR manager of public affairs and government relations, provides hints of the fear which the establishment now holds towards environmental activism. Referring to the benefit concert organized by Ian Tyson in June 1989 to stop the Oldman Dam project in Alberta, Duncan writes:

> Environmental groups grow increasingly more sophisticated in elevating localized issues to the national agenda. And they do it with stunning efficiency: Tyson carried off his star-studded concert for a reported $3,000. He simply called in some Brownie points with his friends. In the polarization that is occurring, debates about job creation and growth are seemingly holding less appeal: the notion of sustainable development, more. Meanwhile the list of environmental victories and (usually) economic dislocation continues to grow: the withdrawal of Uniroyal Chemical Ltd.'s Alar spray and the shutdown of Rancho Seco, the nuclear plant in Sacramento, both occurred within the past two weeks.[5]

While Duncan feels that "there is a lesson here" for politicians and corporations, it is a lesson that the establishment has been learning for several years. As a PR tactic, the "greening" of corporate and governmental personas has been used since at least the late 1970s, when a rash of health- and environment-threatening disasters (Three Mile Island, Love Canal, the Mississauga chlorine-train wreck, increased acid rain) boosted public concern by a quantum leap.

One of the first companies to attempt this particular form of image-revamping also deserves the corporate bullshit award for the 1970s for its advocacy campaign that stated: "When you get right down to it, you'd be hard pressed to find any group of people who care as much about the environmental and economic well-being of Niagara Falls as the people at Hooker Chemical."[6] Having dumped 43.6 million pounds of waste solvents and pesticide residues into

Love Canal from 1942 to 1953, Hooker nevertheless maintains to this day that the resulting toxic mess and health disaster were not its fault.[7]

As Love Canal became household terminology in the late 1970s, Hooker embarked on a nation-wide PR campaign, complete with thousands of glossy pamphlets and a travelling two-man "truth squad", to convince the press and the public of its corporate social conscience. When that tactic failed, the company changed its name to Occidental Chemical, a subsidiary of Occidental Petroleum Corporation, chaired at the time by Armand Hammer.

Public opinion polls conducted by the Ontario government in 1980 revealed that the people of the province felt strongly about the increasing pollution of the Ontario environment as well as the larger ecosystem. In a move characteristic for the time, the government put out a series of ads featuring vignettes of Ontario wilderness areas while an actor sitting in a canoe addressed the TV audience, saying: "I'm an engineer and I work all over the world. Ontario is the cleanest place that I know."[8] Trying to convince us that our perceptions were mistaken proved, however, to be increasingly untenable as the 1980s progressed. Confronted with first-hand evidence of dying lakes and forests, polluted drinking water, closed beaches, droughts and soil erosion, thermal inversions during urban summers, as well as news of fresh disasters like the pesticide leak at the Union Carbide factory in Bhopal, India, the death of the Rhine and the Black Forest, drought and famines in Africa, and the nuclear accident at Chernobyl, the majority of the population proved to have a significant "awareness level" (as the pollster would put it) of the whole environmental issue.

A nation-wide attitudinal survey conducted by Angus Reid in the summer of 1988 – the summer of the PCB fire at St.-Basile-le-Grand, Quebec – revealed that 83 per cent of Canadians ranked the environment as "very important", with 80 per cent willing to spend more for consumer items that are environmentally safe. A whopping 89 per cent believed that private industry does not contribute enough to solving environmental problems. Confronted with this environmentally aware public, corporations and governments began to take some unusual twists as part of a heightened effort to cover their assets. Like Hooker Chemical, McDonald's, and Nestlé's Carnation, they would like us to believe they "care".

□

In early 1988 the B.C. Council of Forest Industries initiated a paradigmatic example of PR "greening". Under attack for hideously irresponsible logging practices, the Council mounted a massive and expensive campaign to convince the public of its "sound forest stewardship and reforestation programs". The campaign included educational displays in shopping malls, huge posters at bus stops, ads inside buses, and colour supplements delivered to most households in the province. As Kalevi Poeg reported, "There is even a $3,000 prize for high school students with the best essays on the theme: Why Clearcut Logging Is Beneficial for British Columbia."[9] The industry also developed a free educational package for B.C. classrooms, including a twenty-minute video presentation and twenty learning modules to "help secondary teachers and students understand our forest resources, the forest industry and what they mean to our province".[10]

But the biggest irritant in the whole PR effort was the Council's "Forests Forever" ads: a $2 million pitch on billboards and TV and in the print media in which Council spokespeople say what a wonderful job they are doing in managing B.C. forests. At the end of each colour TV commercial there is a breathtaking shot of ancient trees bathed in cathedral light while a mellow male voice intones the words "Forests Forever".[11] The ads ran for over a year on CBC-TV despite protests by environmental groups; but when a counter-ad, "Mystical Forests", detailing the actual practices of the logging industry, was proposed by environmentalists and presented for CBC approval, it was turned down as "too controversial". Amidst the storm of protest that resulted from CBC's double standard, the network pulled the "Forests Forever" campaign off the air, but by then the commercial had already received a year's run on the public network. As Kalle Lasn and Bill Schmalz put it, the "Forests Forever" pitch "sounded great – and people believed it".[12]

This incident reveals, among other things, the prevailing ideology among our media institutions. A message in support of the status quo is typically considered to be "neutral", "objective", and "non-controversial", while a message that departs from the status quo position or criticizes it is considered to have a "point of view" and "bias". Recent rulings by the CTRC regarding campus and community radio have reinforced this double standard.

In its decision regarding the license-renewal hearing for CFRO-
FM Co-op Radio in Vancouver in 1988, the CRTC ruled that the station had not achieved "balance" in its programming on "matters of
public concern". At issue in the case was a series of broadcasts called
"The Voice of Palestine" produced by Co-op Radio, but the repercussions of the ruling extended beyond the politics of the Middle East.
During the hearing Co-op Radio took the position that it is the role
of campus and community broadcasters to balance the mainstream
media, arguing that the CRTC's balance requirement station-by-
station "would require us to establish programs that give voices to
sectors of society that already have voices in the [mainstream]
media".[13]

Expressing disagreement, the CRTC reiterated that each station
must achieve "balance", but "not all programming need be bal-
anced, only that relating to matters of public concern".[14] The ambiguity of it all was highlighted by Peter Fleming, Director General of
Radio for the CRTC, who defined "matters of public concern" to
mean "hot topics" such as abortion, capital punishment, foreign policy, and free trade.[15]

As environmental issues increasingly become "matters of public
concern", the CRTC ruling would logically suggest that virtually
every product ad on mainstream radio and TV should be followed by
a counter-ad pointing out the product's health and environmental
dangers in order to achieve "balance". While it is highly doubtful
that the CRTC would ever see the situation in these terms, the argument gains credibility as corporations increasingly tailor their product advertising not only to contain more subtle issues-advocacy but
also to convey (at least on the surface) the new "environmentally
friendly" image. No doubt the CRTC would argue that ads are not
"programming" and thus do not need "balance", though the distinc-
tion is, to my way of thinking, untenable. In terms of conveying the
dominant world-view, ads and programs reinforce one another and
blur together: they both sell us a way of life that has itself become a
"matter of public concern".

☐

Co-opting nature icons for polluting products has been a time-tested
strategy of marketing ever since the industry discovered "Marlboro
Country", but in the late 1980s that tactic assumed new proportions. A sign of the times could be found in an ad campaign for

Craven A cigarettes. Where once upon a time smokers were depicted enjoying the killer weed in great outdoors settings, the company now took a more aggressive stance by actually carving the corporate logo into the landscape. The ads showed smokers on a golf course where the putting green had been mowed into a huge circle containing the words "Craven A", or on a beach where a similar transformation was made of the sandy expanse. The message is like a staking of a land-claim, asserting the corporate place in the landscape, but also asserting the human "need" to rework and transform natural surroundings. In their attitudes towards nature the ads subtly stated that corporations have a right to alter the earth.

Where once car manufacturers were content to utilize animal totems merely in naming their vehicles, more recently the advertising goal was to completely anthropomorphize the product, making it seem like a new "species" and therefore worthy of human and animal rights. For instance, a 1988 ad for Saab in *Harrowsmith* stated that the car was "an heir to the air" — subtly suggesting that automobiles too deserve their share of the available oxygen.

A Nissan Pathfinder ad claimed the vehicle was "half man, half beast", thereby denying all technological reality. Similarly the 1989 Audi ad, with its slogan "the hills are alive", transferred that ecological awareness to the car, making it seem like just another species roaming the planet. Ironically, in the January 2, 1989, edition of *Time,* whose cover story was devoted to the woes of "Endangered Earth", a Mercury Cougar ad made the claim that the car was "the next breed of cat", apparently meant to replace the actual animal species. The copy adopted a pseudo-evolutionary tone: "The breed begins. Again. Sleeker. Faster. More intelligent."

Attributing species status to polluting products like cars apparently allows them to frolic at will in nature. But sometimes advertisers actually proclaim human status for their products. The Hyundai ad for 1989 depicted a car apparently being delivered by stork. The "bundle of joy" will hold claim to its "parents'" loving care and attention no matter how naughty it is to the actual environment. Likewise, a Mercedes-Benz ad claimed that its product was "the automobile every sports sedan wants to be when it grows up".

But sometimes even human status isn't enough for consumer products. Electronics and computer corporations often claim super-species status for their technologies. A 1989 *Maclean's* ad for Gold Star Electronics stated: "To err is human, so Gold Star tests with robots". Move over, humans, your claim to the planet is being usurped.

A November 7, 1988, ad in *Maclean's*, placed by the Canadian Nuclear Association lobby group, showed a family relaxing on the grassy slopes of a park with a nuclear power plant (the Pickering Generating Station) clearly visible in the background. At first one assumes that the ad copy accompanying such a photograph will be decidedly anti-nuclear, since the juxtaposition of this happy nuclear-family outing and the nuclear-power plant is so ironic and bizarre; but the accompanying ad copy is all about the "safety" of nuclear power. Something that does not inherently belong in the landscape and is in fact a major polluter is made to seem like a "natural" feature of the scenic view.

Corporate attempts to naturalize pollution and polluters extend into language use as well. A January 1989 Toyota ad boasted about "performance verging on meltdown" – twisting the meaning of the word into favourable connotations. A Ford Aerostar ad in *Harrowsmith* asserted that it is "a sporty Eddie Bauer model ... with new Eddie Bauer style", as though associations with this outdoor clothing manufacturer might compensate for an otherwise polluting product.

But two of the weirdest "environmental" campaigns in this recent period involved Benson & Hedges and Chrysler Canada. Benson & Hedges, the tobacco giant, had adopted new strategies to provide product appeal. One technique, based on perception reversal, was used in an ad featuring a woman running a comb through her long dark hair; superimposed on her tresses were gold streaks and the Benson & Hedges logo, with the caption "Black and Gold" (the corporate colours). Despite the fact that one of the things people dislike about smoking is its lingering odour on the body and clothing and in the hair, here the company reversed that perception with a seemingly "beautiful" image. In other words, if the nose is offended appeal to the eyes.

Other Benson & Hedges ads took an even more aggressive approach by seemingly tattooing natural species with the logo. One two-page magazine ad showed a beautiful flower being approached by a Monarch butterfly: one flower petal and both butterfly wings are inscribed with the corporate name. While on one level this might seem to be a co-opting of nature iconography and associations, on another level it is a bizarre but bold assertion of nature as corporate enemy: tattooed in advance of extermination.

Chrysler Canada's 1989 marketing campaign took a similar approach. A two-page magazine ad showed a close-up of the red exterior of a car body with raindrops falling on it. The bold ad-copy stated: "Over time, the penetrating force of a single drop of rain will pierce metal like a bullet." At first glance the reader might expect the remaining print of the ad to be devoted to the issue of acid rain, with maybe something about corporate responsibility for helping to diminish the sulphur dioxide emissions from car exhaust. But no, Chrysler takes a different tack, portraying nature as the hostile enemy: "Rain is only the accomplice. The real killer is ferric oxide. The deadly combination of water, air and metal we call rust." The ad went on to talk about the protective coating applied to Chryslers to combat the seeming terrorist aggression of nature and its penetrating "bullets".

But perhaps the biggest irony of the 1989 Chrysler Canada ad campaign was its slogan "Changing The Landscape". No other technology in this century has done more to alter and threaten the planet, with the depletion of fossil fuels, the paving of the earth, the creation of toxic and acid rain devastating our forests and lakes and contributing to the "greenhouse effect" looming on the horizon. In a cynical and bizarre twist, Chrysler Canada's new corporate slogan simultaneously boasted about such effects, incorporated an environmental buzzword, and promised to wreak further havoc. As the ad made clear, the "landscape" Chrysler cares about is the smooth, unpitted, and non-corroded surface of the beloved new car, the only "body" that really counts.

□

B.C. environmentalist John Massey has succinctly named the contemporary situation: "Sometimes it seems that the violence which the resource industries do to our lands and forests is matched only by that which they do to our mother tongue."[16] No doubt everyone has a favourite example of what Massey calls "weasel words", but for me it is the public-relations pitch mounted by GRANDCO – Thomas Kierans's consortium dedicated to diverting Canadian fresh water from a proposed James Bay dam through a 167-mile canal to Georgian Bay, where it is to be flushed through the Great Lakes and piped down to the U.S. sunbelt.[17] This idea, promoted behind closed doors by Ottawa public-affairs specialists such as Arthur Bailey and Duncan Edmonds (the latter with connections to PAI, the most powerful public-affairs consulting company in the country), is being called an "environmental" solution to water shortages through its "water recycling" program.

But perhaps even GRANDCO has been topped by the "environmental" efforts of Viceroy Resources Corporation of Vancouver. In 1989 the mining company proposed a 900-acre gold mine in the mountainous part of the U.S. Mojave Desert, an area already designated a national scenic area and soon to be a national park. Since such designations no longer hinder resource development, Viceroy made its pitch to U.S. Secretary of the Interior Manuel Lujan. Included were plans to dye its cyanide-laced tailings brown so that they look like desert sand. After a tour of the site in May 1989 the Secretary of the Interior told reporters that he was impressed with "the natural look" of the dyed tailings.[18]

It was by such loathsome manoeuvrings that the whole "reformist" posture of the born-again "green" establishment revealed its real agenda. In the effort to prevent radical change, its manipulation of the public's environmental awareness achieved new depths.

In 1987 a survey conducted for the Canadian Nuclear Association (CNA) revealed that only 15 per cent of the public strongly favoured nuclear power. The leaked minutes of an April 1987 CNA economic development committee meeting stated, "In order to regain political clout, this [public perception] must be turned around."[19] The CNA – a lobby group representing more than one hundred companies and government agencies – subsequently launched its three-year, $6 million "public information program" to improve the image of nuclear power, especially in light of other environmental factors. Casting nuclear energy as the "clean" and "safe" energy path for the future as well as a "solution" to concerns such as the greenhouse effect and acid rain, the CNA would like us to think of the nuclear industry as a "green" alternative to burning coal, oil, and natural gas.

Its public-relations program extended beyond TV ads and two-page colour spreads in mainstream magazines. The CNA provided materials and speakers for classrooms. CNA vice-president Ian Wilson said, "We look at grade 10 and 11 classes in science that are being introduced to concepts such as energy and nuclear power."[20] This classroom effort buttressed the school programs long conducted by the AECL and Ontario Hydro. In the late 1980s Atomic Energy of Canada Ltd. spent nearly $30,000 per year to send speakers to schools across the country, while Ontario Hydro had four full-time teachers working out of its Bruce and Darlington nuclear plants. As usual, a double standard is in effect. Anti-nuclear groups say that they are usually not allowed to distribute their materials in schools and do not have the resources to compete with the nuclear industry in any case.[21]

This public-relations effort is taking place world-wide, as nuclear proponents recognize a new window of opportunity in the growing environmental crisis. Nobel Prize winner Carlo Rubbia, head of the Geneva-based European Centre for Nuclear Research, has declared, "New forms of nuclear power may be the only way to save the world from the devastating impact of the 'greenhouse effect'."[22] Speaking at the World Economic Forum in February 1989, Rubbia urged massive investment to develop new fusion reactors considered "safer" and more powerful than the existing technology. His audience of a thousand international business and political leaders in attendance at the week-long conference may well have been reassured by Rubbia's claim: "I believe that the research efforts on fusion must be pursued and encouraged since they hold real promise to solve one of the most crucial problems of the future of mankind, namely its long range energy supply."[23]

The idea that nuclear power "can save the world" is being reinforced by current cost-benefit analyses that "prove" that nuclear electricity is cheaper than its coal-fired counterpart. On April 4, 1989, Ontario energy minister Bob Wong released the Nuclear Cost Inquiry Panel's report, which concluded that "Ontario Hydro's nuclear cost estimates are an appropriate basis to compare energy options". On that basis, Wong told reporters, "A new nuclear generating station is clearly a possibility. The existing nuclear stations produce about half of our electricity, efficiently and safely."[24] Meanwhile the cost of Ontario Hydro's new Darlington nuclear power station, set to start up in September 1989, had reached $12.5 billion according to a Hydro press release of June 1.[25]

The supposed "renaissance" being predicted for nuclear technology is predicated on several prevailing assumptions within the industry. At the 1989 annual meeting of the Canadian Nuclear Association the conference was told that "A 'staggering' need for electricity in developed and developing countries, worry about pollution from fossil fuels, better technology, and *a softening of public and political opposition* will pave the way back to nuclear energy in the coming years."[26] Thus, only three years after Chernobyl, the industry was counting on what environmental writer Kenneth Brower termed perhaps "the greatest environmental threat of all: the short attention span of modern man".[27] As well, it was relying on the "softening" of political opposition, presumably through co-opting the environmental movement around the issue of the economy.

In June 1989, Colin Isaacs of the oppositional environmental group Pollution Probe stirred up a controversy with his commercial endorsement of Loblaw's line of one hundred "Green products". Isaacs, Pollution Probe's executive director, appeared on TV commercials with Loblaw's president Dave Nichol extolling the virtues and value of the supermarket chain's products. In the mounting furore that led up to Isaacs' resignation, perhaps the most interesting perspective was expressed by Dave Nichol:

> Environmental groups have always sat on the sidelines carping and complaining. *And under that scenario, nothing ever happened.* Colin has been the first to break down the old role models of us being the bad guys and them being the white knights. His genius was in realizing the enormous power of the consumer to cause change by voting at the checkout. But someone had to produce the products, didn't they?[28] [my emphasis]

Nichol's questionable assertion that "nothing ever happened" as a result of environmental groups' "carping and complaining" was an attempt to depict Loblaw's as the new white knight of environmental activism. Beyond the question of whether or not Loblaw's new Green Line of disposable diapers was really "biodegradable", or whether or not its Green Line of lawn fertilizer was really "toxic", is the larger question of what real change means.

Arguably, Nichol's assertion must be understood in the light of former Shell PR man Stephen Duncan's veiled warning in *The Financial Post* that, as justifications for environmental degradation, "job creation and growth are seemingly holding less appeal" for the public. Corporations and governments have recognized that the radical perspective in environmental politics has gained momentum, especially as establishment PR "greens" itself and degrades the very word "environmentalist". A 1986 survey conducted in the United States for the Sierra Club revealed not only that 60 per cent of the U.S. public considered themselves to be "very sympathetic" to the goals of the environmental movement, but also that (even more clarifying) nearly 40 per cent considered themselves to be "hard-core" environmentalists – they said they "favor environmental goals regardless of their cost to the economy".[29] It is this political position that has caused the most fear and loathing within corporate and governmental sectors. It has also led to splits inside the environmental movement throughout the past decade.

New actionist groups like Earth First! (whose rallying cry is "No compromise in defense of Mother Earth!") and more than seventy other bioregional activist groups have sprung up across the continent over the last ten years. Most eschew the word "environmentalist" and criticize the major conservationist and environmental groups on a range of issues. Author Kirkpatrick Sale, writing for *Mother Jones*, clustered those issues into four major themes:

1. Environmentalists are reformist, working within "the system" in ways that ultimately reinforce it instead of seeking the thoroughgoing social and political changes that are necessary to halt massive assaults on the natural world.... 2. Environmentalists are basically anthropocentric, believing that the proper human purpose is to control and consume the resources of nature as wisely and safely – but as fully – as possible. They have yet to learn the ecocentric truth that nature and all its species have an intrinsic worth apart from any human designs.... 3. Environmentalists have become co-opted into the world of Washington politics, playing the bureaucratic game like any other lobby, turning their backs on the grass roots support and idealism that gave the movement its initial momentum.... 4. Environmentalists, finally, are not successful even on their own terms in protecting the wilderness, in stopping the onrush of industrial devastation. They are so caught up in compromise that they're actually going backward.[30]

These charges form the basis for delineating the differences between reformist and radical perspectives. They have become especially pertinent in the wake of the Brundtland Report with its new buzzword and rallying cry of "sustainable development".

Established by the UN General Assembly in 1983, the World Commission on Environment and Development, chaired by Norway's Prime Minister Gro Harlem Brundtland, was asked to formulate "a global agenda for change" to deal with the increasing environmental crisis. That agenda was released in the Commission's

1987 report *Our Common Future*.[31] It is not coincidental that within a year of the report's publication the political leaders of virtually all overdeveloped countries had become born-again environmentalists. The Brundtland Report provided an "environmental" platform that threatens no one and nothing but the planet itself.

□

In 1980, Gro Brundtland was a member of the Brandt Commission on North-South Issues established by Robert McNamara as president of the World Bank. The Brandt Commission's report, *North-South: A Programme for Survival*, was supposedly an in-depth analysis of the international economy, leading to calls for increased aid to alleviate Third World poverty. The Brandt Report and its mostly uncritical reception prompted Teresa Hayter to write "an alternative view to the Brandt Report" entitled *The Creation of World Poverty*.[32] The Brandt Report, wrote Hayter, "like most of the orthodox literature on development, notably omits to explain why the [Third World] poverty exists in the first place. If it attempted such an explanation, it might come to the embarrassing conclusion that the poverty is caused precisely by the economic system which its proposals are supposed to protect".[33]

Filling in much of the history of the industrialized world's plundering of Third World countries as well as providing a detailed analysis of contemporary events like the Green Revolution and the creation of export processing zones and free trade zones, Hayter asserted that the authors of the Brandt Commission Report were "primarily concerned with the preservation of the existing world economic order":

> There are nevertheless two important differences between the current and previous states of establishment opinion: first, extreme poverty in underdeveloped countries is now seen as a real threat to the survival of the system rather than as something to be dealt with by occasional philanthropic gestures; and, second, a response is required to the current crisis in the world economy.[34]

Similar charges can be made of the Brundtland report, *Our Common Future*, especially that it is primarily concerned with the "preservation of the existing world economic order". A detailed critique of the report is needed, particularly of the notion of "sustainable development". While such an extended analysis is not possible in the context of this text, it is nevertheless useful to discuss a number of the assumptions that are evident in *Our Common Future*, assumptions that make it so readily embraceable by corporate and governmental spokespersons.

The Brundtland Report makes it perfectly clear that it is committed to "more rapid economic growth in both industrial and developing countries ... the international economy must speed up world growth while respecting the environmental constraints".[35] In other words, as the report asserts, "sustainable development is *not a fixed state of harmony*, but rather a process of change in which the exploitation of resources, the direction of investments, the orientation of technological development, and institutional change are made consistent with future as well as present needs."[36] Behind this thinking is the assumption that nature is to be perceived as "resources" and that those exist entirely for human use. Thus: "The genetic variability and germplasm material of species make contributions to agriculture, medicine, and industry worth many billions of dollars per year.... This – the scope for species to make a fast-growing contribution to human welfare in myriad forms – is a major justification for expanded efforts to safeguard Earth's millions of species."[37] This anthropocentric position is "necessary" because the Commission foresees "the possibility for a new era of economic growth, one that must be based on policies that sustain and expand the environmental resource base".[38]

This expansion is to be accomplished through the Commission's unquestioning belief in the technological fix, especially in biotechnology which is endorsed throughout the report, but in all technologies in general, which are said to be nothing less than "the key link between humans and nature".[39] With regard to limits to growth: "The concept of sustainable development does imply limits – not absolute limits but limitations imposed by the present state of technology and social organization on environmental resources and by the ability of the biosphere to absorb the effects of human activities. But technology and social organization can be both managed and improved to make way for a new era of economic growth."[40] So intent is the Commission on not offending the aspirations of technocrats that it virtually endorses the concept of nuclear reactors in orbit, provided they are limited in size and shielded to withstand re-entry into the Earth's atmosphere.[41]

The other prevailing hope of the Commission is the role of transnational corporations. *Our Common Future* emphatically asserts
that the multinationals need to "play a larger role in development"
and "have a special responsibility to smooth the path of industrialization in the nations in which they operate".[42] To do this, the Commission warns that in the relationship between large corporations
and small developing countries "conflicts and suspicions must be
reduced".[43] Obviously avoiding the whole issue of multinationals'
history in the Third World – a history that provides no reason to
expect responsible action in environmental terms or, for that matter,
in economic terms – the Brundtland Report must place its hope in
the multinationals to preserve the existing economic order. The
paradox of such a position is only enhanced by a variety of other
highly questionable views.

With regard to non-renewable fossil fuels and minerals the Commission recommends that "the rate of depletion and the emphasis
on recycling and economy of use should be calibrated to ensure that
the resource does not run out before acceptable substitutes are available."[44] Nevertheless, while warning that "ultimate limits there
are", the Commission's concept of sustainability "requires that long
before these are reached, the world must ensure equitable access to
the constrained resource".[45] This belief that it is ecologically sound
to use up a non-renewable resource is highly questionable, given
that scientists know so little about the subtle roles that core minerals and fuels inside the Earth play in maintaining larger systems like
the Earth's electromagnetic field. But such subtleties are beyond the
thinking of the Brundtland Report, which opts for a highly utilitar-
ian approach.

Indeed, its tone is at times simply anti-ecological. For example:
"The use of agricultural chemicals is not in itself harmful. In fact,
the level of use is still quite low in many regions. In these areas,
response rates are high and the environmental consequences of residues are not yet a problem. Hence these regions would benefit by
using more agrochemicals."[46] Similarly: "Many countries can and
should increase yields by greater use of chemical fertilizers and pes-
ticides, particularly in the developing world."[47] And with regard to
non-renewable minerals the report reassures that "recent assess-
ments suggest that few minerals are likely to run out in the near
future."[48] This attitude – that where there is not yet a problem irresponsible practices may be followed until there is one – is part of the

reason that "sustainable development" has been so warmly received in corporate circles. As well, the Commission holds out the illusion that "the progress that some have known over the last century can be experienced by all in the years ahead".[49]

In general, the Brundtland Report tries desperately to offend nobody, especially economic powers, while appearing to be "environmentally friendly" in scope. The contradictions that result can be summarized by one of the report's baldest statements: "Governments can stem the destruction of the tropical forests and other reservoirs of biological diversity while developing them economically."[50] Arguably, this is the kind of "communications" they must teach in public-relations school, but it no doubt serves its purpose for the UN, which promoted the multinationals-based economy in the first place.

As David Suzuki writes:

Global economics now dominates the world, and governments are driven by the overriding priority to maximize growth in GNP, consumption and wealth ... the very definition of progress. But a direct consequence of this economic imperative is environmental degradation. Economics makes no ecological sense because it fails to account for the necessity to recycle finite supplies of air, water and soil or to posit worth to intact ecosystems and their many "services" such as cleansing the air, retarding erosion, etc.[51]

The Brundtland Report makes little ecological sense and perhaps in the long run little economic sense, since its concept of "progress" is essentially unchanged from the economic boosterism of the 1950s: "Our report, Our Common Future, is not a prediction of ever increasing environmental decay, poverty, and hardship in an ever more polluted world among ever decreasing resources. We see instead the possibility for a new era of economic growth, one that must be based on policies that sustain and expand the environmental resource base."[52] Stephanie Cairns, former national co-ordinator of the Canadian Environmental Network, refers to the report as "having our message 'airbrushed'" and warns:

The lexicon we mustn't abandon is one of holocaust. A growing number of horrified scientists are warning us that we face an ecological

crisis.... Forget the nuance of whether your toddler wears "biodegradable" or regular disposable diapers. We're questioning whether tod-
dlers will even be able to play in the ultraviolet radiation-laden sunlight in 50 years. If we succumb to using the vocabulary of "opportunity" and "challenge", we lose the capacity to convey the critical
urgency of our message. Only by painting things as they are – desperate – will we arouse the massive awakening and changes needed to
brake our fall towards annihilation.[53]

By 1988 that "hole" in the ozone layer was bigger than continental
U.S.A. and still growing, with some scientists beginning to suspect
that nuclear radiation was a significant factor in the problem. Moreover, the dovetailing of numerous environmental stresses indicated
a looming crisis much bigger than any one problem considered on its
own, a situation that Cairns accurately calls "desperate". No doubt
to Loblaw's president Dave Nichol and other establishment born-
again "environmentalists" this is just another example of the usual
"carping and complaining".

In July 1989 the leaders of the Group of Seven nations ended their
economic summit in Paris by devoting about a third of their final
communiqué to environmental concerns. Craig McInnes reported,
"The summit leaders recommended strongly that action be taken to
tackle the problems, but stopped short of committing themselves to
any specific programs or timetables for action."[54] In response to the
G-7 summit's "green veneer" Joyce McLean of Greenpeace com-
mented, "People in the environmental community are happy to see
the issue being discussed at such a summit, but it's going to take
more than just talk and rhetoric to remedy the problems that we're
dealing with."[55]

Talk and rhetoric, however, do win awards. On May 4, 1989, the
Prime Minister of Canada received special recognition from the
International Chamber of Commerce for his "environmental
achievements". Casting back over the Mulroney years, it is difficult
to think of what the ICC had in mind unless it was Mulroney's
supreme efforts to create that necessary "favourable business environment" through the free trade deal. Most recently, the Mulroney
government had budgeted $5.1 billion in 1989 for loans and grants to
extract fossil fuel resources in Canada over a period of five years,
while budgeting only $160 million for alternative energy sources for
the same period.[56] In this the government was perhaps heeding the

Brundtland Report which, with regard to solar energy sources, warns of "their health and environment risks", including "the injuries from roof falls during solar thermal maintenance".[57]

The new "green veneer" with which Thatcher, Bush, and Mulroney have been painting themselves should remind us of those cyanide-laced gold-mine tailings that Viceroy Resources Corporation proposed to dye brown for "the natural look". Their PR rhetoric is toxic, a form of mind pollution. As Peggy Hallward, forestry researcher for Probe International, put it, "My huge fear is that the public will sigh a huge sigh of relief and say 'great, the leaders finally understand the mess we're in' and yet we still finance and give huge subsidies to all the fossil fuel projects."[58] But, as the Brundtland Report explained, "As for non-renewable resources, like fossil fuels and minerals, their use reduces the stock available for future generations. But this does not mean that such resources should not be used.... Sustainable development requires that the rate of depletion of non-renewable resources should foreclose as few future options as possible."[59] No wonder "sustainable development" is rapidly becoming the buzzword of choice in corporate boardrooms across the world. It really *does* mean sustained development and the continued altering of the ecosystem to suit human greed. "Economic growth and development obviously involve changes in the physical ecosystem. Every ecosystem everywhere cannot be preserved intact. A forest may be depleted in one part of a watershed and extended elsewhere, *which is not a bad thing if the exploitation has been planned* and the effects on soil erosion rates, water regions, and genetic losses have been taken into account."[60] Preferable to the bafflegab in *Our Common Future* is the wisdom of a current scrawl on the wall: "A good planet is hard to find".

Triage: A Brief Conclusion

Where traditions and values are destroyed or in abeyance, the
ground from which momentous changes are nurtured and grow
– the power to decide, to change course, to redirect personal
and social commitment, even to remember the suffering of
others – becomes sterile and dry. The power of modernity has
only one greater enemy than itself: the resurgence of an imagination to make conscious our suffering and to redirect the
movement of the world.

MARC H. ELLIS

IN HIS POWERFUL book *Faithfulness in an Age of Holocaust,*
Marc Ellis – who has worked for years with the homeless and the
poor of the United States, Latin America, the Middle East, and Asia –
recognizes the "paradoxical mingling of progress and holocaust"
that characterizes this century. This state of affairs, he argues, has
resulted not just in massive uprootedness and homelessness for hundreds of millions of people around the world but in so-called "acceptable levels" of every other kind of tragedy as well, including mass
death when it can be "justified" by the politics of "progress". Such
"crimes of logic" occur daily – whether it is through mercury and
dioxin poisoning of indigenous peoples, the dispossession of land
claims, "acceptable levels" of radiation and chemical contamina-
tions, the extinction of more than ten thousand species each year, or
the "disappearing" of political opponents. "Such a world," Ellis
writes, "necessitates special types of people who dwell in abstrac-
tion and power, intelligent people who can create and maintain a
complex society but who are, in essence, alienated from emotion
and compassion".[1]

Michael Brown, author of *Laying Waste: The Poisoning of*

America by Toxic Chemicals, provides a vivid example of triage in action. In the wake of the Love Canal, the New York state government's Department of Health conducted a risk / benefit analysis to estimate the financial value of saving people from exposure to toxic wastes. According to Brown:

> A key section of the 130-page draft, subtitled "The Benefit of Reducing Risk," contained six empirical estimates of what a life means financially to society, figures culled in large part from other governmental literature. "Estimates range from $49,226 to $1 million with most values between $200,000 and $300,000," it said coolly. "These estimates will be used later to describe the benefit of reducing the risk of death."[2]

Part of the basis for estimating the financial value of a life was "the worth of an individual's present production", though the report admitted the weakness in such a methodology because it would "undervalue lives of housewives, elderly, unemployed, and underemployed," and provide "no allowance ... for social values or the utility of life to an individual".[3] Nevertheless, writes Brown:

> The report went on to conclude that whenever trichloroethylene was greater than fifty parts per billion in drinking water, based on a risk of one extra death in a population of 100,000 and an assumed economic life value of $500,000, it would be worthwhile to install aeration treatment to decrease contaminant levels in a system serving ten million gallons a day, but that "treatment of smaller systems cannot be justified based on these data." Therefore individuals who owned their own wells or who were attached to small municipal systems would not, based on economic considerations, be provided the proper protection.[4]

Triage – the systematic "culling" and dismissal of peoples and species deemed peripheral or superfluous to some larger agenda – is the underlying *Zeitgeist* that has replaced many other values as the basis for society. It is directly linked to an economy in which "worth" is judged by monetary standards alone. The perspective expressed in the New York state government's risk / benefit report is accepted as "realistic" rather than cynical, "reasonable" rather than morally bankrupt.

It is a harsh statement to make, but in many ways the mainstream public-relations industry has proved itself to be at the forefront of a century of triage. By providing whitewashed personas for the most dubious of governments, corporations, and marketing goals, as well as arranging the necessary deals behind closed doors, the industry reveals its own shadow-side as the sultans of sleaze. Given some of the PR campaigns explored in this text, the title actually lets them off lightly.

It must be said, however, that the ideology of triage is not entirely new. After all, during three centuries of the slave trade well over 60 million black people died in the slave-ships alone; during the first century of white settlement of North America more than 17 million native people were killed; and it is estimated that 12 million women were killed as "witches" during three centuries of persecution. Extermination of "marginal" people is nothing new in human history.

But what is new in this century is a powerful system of mass media interlocked with a technological and economic agenda that now threatens the entire planet. The paradox we face is that our lifestyle of luxury and "progress" – promulgated through the media over this century – increasingly reveals itself to be the prescription for planetary suicide. Moreover, that media system – which McLuhan referred to as the externalized nervous system of humanity – does not function to alert us to problems as soon as they are known, but instead is purposely controlled and used to keep us uninformed of critical problems, or misinformed about their causes and repercussions, and reassured that nothing needs to change.

But a growing number of people are beginning to reject the dominant lifestyle and "values" and are engaged in redefining the prevailing concepts of "rich" and "poor". Choosing and exploring a wide variety of paths based on voluntary simplicity and social activism, people are returning to their imaginations, ingenuity, and skills to find solutions for living their daily lives according to basic needs rather than created needs, and in harmony with the Earth. This return includes the re-learning of older ways for doing things – an effort that is going to become even more crucial as the health hazards of electric power lines and even electric appliances are revealed.

After more than twenty years of controversy in the scientific field, this issue finally hit the mainstream in 1989, with articles in both *The New Yorker* and *Time* magazine discussing the effects of technologically-generated electromagnetic fields on human health, effects that may include suppression of the immune system, childhood leukemia, and other forms of cancer. As *Time* put it, the research implications "could be devastating. Appliances and electronic equipment would have to be redesigned, many homes rewired, and the nation's power-distribution system overhauled. Lawsuits, already on the rise, would surge as citizens filed claims to cover illness or property devaluation."[5] It is largely because of these repercussions that the issue has been kept out of the mainstream media for so long. In his three-part article for *The New Yorker* Paul Brodeur documents the extraordinary public-relations effort conducted by the utilities, other corporations, trade associations, and lobby groups to keep this issue under wraps.[6]

Similarly, the mounting garbage problem directly implicates our consumer culture. While the Brundtland Report upholds the idea of "producing more with less", it applies this to industry – where already the surfeit of unnecessary consumer products and packaging is drowning the world in garbage. Breaking away from both the fashion industry and the product industry based on built-in obsolescence and disposable items will involve a major shift in values, indeed in "wealth" itself. When people no longer define their worth and status in terms of owning the "latest", or the "newest", or the "most convenient", significant shifts in the entire economy will take place, especially in local efforts to meet local needs.

It is often said that "we can't go back to the past", an expression that usually means the modern multinationals-based economy is so completely dependent on maintaining the status quo that alternative or older ways of living would undermine it and throw it into chaos. Besides the fact that the global economy is already in chaos, the practices upon which it is based are politically, morally, and environmentally bankrupt. Indeed, that is why such a tremendous public-relations effort is put into maintaining the status quo – a redoubling of rhetoric and photo-ops, cosmetic "change", and meaningless gestures meant to keep us from using our own imaginations to find radical alternatives. It is well to remember that "radical" change means change "at the root". As Marc Ellis observes, that "*ground* from which momentous changes are nurtured and grow" has become "sterile and dry" and needs a "resurgence of imagination". Here, each one of us can play our part: we can begin by reclaiming our imaginations, which have been colonized by a century of PR geared to "regimenting the public mind". As a first step, that in itself would be a radical break.

Notes

1. Introduction: The Image Brokers

1. Ogilvy & Mather Public Relations, "Pro-active Neutralization: Nestlé Recommendations Regarding the Infant Formula Boycott", excerpted in "Corporate Cointelpro", *Harper's*, July 1989, pp. 24-25.
2. Interview with Prakesh Sethi, University of Texas professor of business, spring 1982, Toronto.
3. John Sawatsky, *The Insiders: Power, Money, and Secrets in Ottawa* (Toronto: McClelland and Stewart, 1989), p. 350.
4. Interview with Morris Wolfe, winter 1981, Toronto.

2. The Time of the Hangman

1. Quoted in Eduardo Galeano, *Memory of Fire*, vol. 3: *Century of the Wind* (New York: Pantheon Books, 1988), p. 233.
2. Cited in Noam Chomsky and Edward S. Herman, *The Political Economy of Human Rights*, vol. 1: *The Washington Connection and Third World Fascism* (Montreal: Black Rose Books, 1979), pp. 266-267.
3. Galeano, p. 233.
4. Jacobo Timerman, speech delivered at the Writer and Human Rights conference, October 1981, Toronto.
5. Quotations in this and following paragraphs are from an interview with Harold Burson, autumn 1981, New York.
6. Chomsky and Herman, pp. 265-266.
7. Quoted in ibid., p. 266.
8. Ed Harriman and Peter Chippendale, *Juntas United!* (London: Quartet Books, 1978), pp. 14-15.
9. Ibid., p. 9.
10. Quoted in ibid., pp. 11 and 14.
11. Cited in ibid., p. 11.
12. Galeano, p. 240.
13. Quotations in this and following paragraphs are from "Report from Burson Marsteller to the Argentine Government re: Improving the International Image of Argentina", circulated by Amnesty International, 1978.
14. Interview with Alexander Craig, autumn 1981, Toronto.
15. See *Canadian Business*, February 1977.
16. See *The Financial Post*, December 11, 1976.

17. Ibid.
18. Chomsky and Herman, p. 263.
19. Jacobo Timerman, *Prisoner Without a Name, Cell Without a Number* (New York: Alfred A. Knopf, 1981), p. 23.
20. Timerman, speech.
21. Quoted in Chomsky and Herman, p. 266.
22. Galeano, p. 238.
23. Timerman, *Prisoner*, p. 33.
24. Andrew Pollack, report for "Sunday Morning", CBC Radio, May 1978 (CBC Archives, Toronto).
25. George Young, report for "CBC Sports", CBC Radio, May 1978 (CBC Archives, Toronto).
26. Timerman, speech.
27. Ibid.
28. Chomsky and Herman, p. 262.
29. Timerman, speech.
30. Ed Harriman, *Hack: Home Truths about Foreign News* (London: Zed Books, 1987), p. 169.
31. Chomsky and Herman, p. 270.
32. Ibid., p. 293.
33. Quoted in Galeano, p. 246.
34. Harriman and Chippendale, p. 97.
35. Chomsky and Herman, p. 283.
36. Harriman and Chippendale, p. 97.
37. Julia Preston, "Killing Off the News in Guatemala", *Columbia Journalism Review*, January 1982.
38. Harriman, p. 143.
39. Preston.
40. Interview with Cameron Smith, autumn 1981, Toronto.
41. Interview with Andrew Weil, autumn 1981, New York.
42. Interview with Curtis Hoxtar, president of Hoxtar Public Relations Inc., autumn 1981, New York.

3. Handling the Legitimacy Gap

1. Doug Newsom and Alan Scott, *This Is PR: The Realities of Public Relations* (New York: Wadsworth Publishing Company, 1976).
2. Interview with Jerry Wattel, president of Hill and Knowlton, autumn 1981, New York.
3. Interview with John O'Connor, autumn 1981, Toronto.
4. Interviews with Norm Rubin, autumn 1981 and May 1989, Toronto.
5. Ibid.
6. O'Connor interview.
7. Rubin interview.
8. See Joyce Nelson, *The Colonized Eye: Rethinking the Grierson Legend* (Toronto: Between The Lines, 1988), pp. 16-26.
9. Alan Raucher, *Public Relations and Business from 1900 to 1929* (Baltimore: Johns Hopkins Press, 1968), p. 33.
10. Jamie Swift, *The Big Nickel: Inco at Home and Abroad* (Toronto: Between The Lines, 1977).

11. Milton Moskowitz, Michael Katz, and Robert Levering, eds., *Everybody's Business: An Almanac* (San Francisco: Harper & Row, 1980), pp. 78-80.

12. Taped interview with Edward Bernays conducted by the Public Relations Society of America, circa 1980.

13. Quoted in Raucher, p. 42.

14. Quoted in Daniel J. Boorstin, *The Image: A Guide to Pseudo-Events in America* (New York: Atheneum, 1972), p. 11.

15. Interviews with Stan Houston, autumn 1981 and May 1989, Toronto.

16. Mark Hertsgaard, "On Bended Knee", *New Age Journal*, March / April 1989, p. 42.

17. Linda McQuaig, *Behind Closed Doors* (Markham, Ont.: Penguin, 1987), p. 315.

18. Interview with Cameron Smith, spring 1982, Toronto.

19. Boorstin, p. 29. Boorstin's text was first published in 1961.

20. Ibid., p. 12.

21. Fred C. Dobbs, *The Golden Age of B.S.* (Markham, Ont.: Paperjacks, 1976).

22. Interview with Carol McIntyre, May 1989, Toronto.

23. Interview with Steve Rowan, autumn 1981, Toronto.

24. Houston interview.

25. Interview with Larry Newman, partner in Manning, Selvage and Lee Communications Inc., autumn 1981, New York.

26. John Sawatsky, *The Insiders: Power, Money, and Secrets in Ottawa* (Toronto: McClelland and Stewart, 1987).

27. McQuaig.

28. Randall Poe, "Masters of the Advertorial", *Across the Board* (The Conference Board of Canada magazine), September 1980, p. 19.

29. Mobil ad, 1980.

30. Mobil ad, 1981.

31. Quoted in Poe, p. 23.

32. Kaiser Aluminum ad, 1980.

33. United Technologies ad, 1981.

34. Interview with Prakesh Sethi, University of Texas, winter 1981, Toronto.

35. Ibid.

36. Ibid.

37. Quoted in Poe, p. 19.

38. *Fortune*, December 1980.

39. *The Globe and Mail*, 1980.

40. Interview with Morris Wolfe, spring 1982, Toronto.

41. Haughton Group ad, 1980.

42. Imperial Oil ad, 1981.

43. Bank of Montreal ad, 1981.

44. Imperial Oil ad, 1981.

45. Bank of Nova Scotia ad, 1982.

46. McQuaig, p. 195.

47. *Saturday Night* ad, 1981.

48. See Joyce Nelson, "The Power of PR", *This Magazine*, August 1984, pp. 17-19.

49. Interview with Herb Schmertz, autumn 1981, New York.

50. Quoted in Hertsgaard, p. 42.

51. See Nelson, "Power", p. 19.

52. Hertsgaard, p. 42.

53. *The Globe and Mail*, May 12, 1984.

54. McQuaig, p. xvii.

55. Linda Diebel, "Wilson Hires Pair of Troubleshooters to Sell Budget Measures to the Public", *The Toronto Star*, April 11, 1989, p. A9.
56. Quoted in Linda Diebel, "Tories Launching Advertising Blitz to Sell Budget Cuts", *The Toronto Star*, May 3, 1989, p. A14.
57. Jean Baudrillard, *Simulations* (New York: Semiotext(e), 1983), p. 126.

4. The Power of the Pollsters

1. Quoted in Ross Laver, "The New Tricks in an Old Trade", *Maclean's*, October 31, 1988, p. 18.
2. Tony Schwartz, *The Responsive Chord* (Garden City, N.Y.: Anchor Books, 1973), p. 82.
3. Telephone interview with Allan Gregg, April 1989, Toronto.
4. John Sawatsky, *The Insiders: Power, Money, and Secrets in Ottawa* (Toronto: McClelland and Stewart, 1989), pp. 149-150.
5. Interview with Steve Rowan, autumn 1981, Toronto.
6. Sawatsky, p. 150.
7. Linda McQuaig, *Behind Closed Doors* (Markham, Ont.: Penguin Books, 1987), p. 62.
8. Jean Baudrillard, *Simulations* (New York: Semiotext(e), 1983), p. 126.
9. Ibid.
10. Kevin Doyle, editorial, *Maclean's*, January 2, 1989, p. 1.
11. Quoted in Sawatsky, p. 147.
12. Roland Perry, *Hidden Power* (New York: Beaufort Books, 1984).
13. Will Ellsworth-Jones and Roland Perry, "The Man Who Programs the President", *The Toronto Star*, May 6, 1984.
14. Quoted in ibid.
15. Perry, p. 42.
16. See Joyce Nelson, "Democracy Incorporated", *The New Internationalist*, April 1985.
17. Sawatsky, p. 147.
18. Katherine Govier, "Polling Alan Gregg", *Toronto Life*, July 1985, p. 70.
19. Sawatsky, p. 151.
20. Nick Fillmore, "The Big Oink: How Business Swallowed Politics", *This Magazine*, March-April 1989, p. 14.
21. Quoted in James Bagnall and Hyman Solomon, "How the Tories Turned the Tide", *The Financial Post*, November 28, 1988, Sec. 2, p. 1.
22. Quoted in ibid.
23. Ibid.
24. Mary Janigan and Hilary McKenzie, "Anatomy of an Election", *Maclean's*, December 5, 1988, p. 24.
25. Quoted in ibid.
26. *The Toronto Star*, October 27, 1988.
27. Quoted in *The Toronto Star*, October 29, 1988.
28. Quoted in Fillmore, p. 14.
29. See Joyce Nelson, "Real Men on the Campaign Trail", *Broadside*, February 1989.
30. Quoted in Janigan and McKenzie, p. 24.
31. Peter Koprillem, "Prime Time for a Blitz of Ads", *Maclean's*, October 31, 1988.
32. Quoted in *The Toronto Star*, November 1, 1988.
33. Quoted in *The Toronto Star*, November 1, 1988.
34. Fillmore, p. 15.
35. Ibid., p. 14.
36. Ibid., p. 16.

37. Theresa Tedesco, "Outside Influences: Business Buys a Powerful Voice", *Maclean's*, December 5, 1988, p. 26.
38. Interview with David Langille, winter 1988, Toronto.
39. *Social Policy Reform and the National Agenda* (Ottawa: BCNI, December 1986).

5. Multinational Free Lunch

1. Charles W. Lindsay, "The Philippine State and Transnational Investment", *Bulletin of Concerned Asian Scholars* vol. 19, no. 2 (1987), p. 40; see also Charles Pasual and Jessica Rayes-Cantos, "Philippines: Reviving the Economy", *Third World Network Features* (1987).
2. Quoted in *Women Workers in Asia* (Hong Kong: CCIA-URM, 1981), p. 11. Other sources relied on for information about Third World zones are: "Silicon Slaves: Women in Malaysia", *Third World Women's News*, vol. 1, no. 1 (1986); Mimi Maduro, "Women, Technology and the Global Economy", *Woman of Power*, fall 1988; "Changing Role of Southeast Asia Women", *Southeast Asia Chronicle*, Jan.-Feb. 1979; Ed Bloch, "Trade and Unemployment: Global Bread-and-Butter Issues", *Monthly Review*, vol. 35, no. 5 (October 1983); "Free Trade Zones: A Capitalist Dream", *Race & Class*, vol. 22 (autumn 1980); *Asian Action*, Nov.-Dec. 1983; Elizabeth Cheng, "Special Economic Zones Face Fight for Capital", *Far Eastern Economic Review*, March 24, 1988; "The Electronics Industry: In Canada, Southeast Asia", *Canadian Asia Currents*, February 1981; Annette Fuentes and Barbara Ehrenreich, *Women in the Global Factory* (Boston: South End Press, 1983); Wendy McKeen, "Export Processing Zones: A Threat to Women, Unions and All Canadian Workers", research paper prepared for the Women's Bureau of the Canadian Labour Congress, 1984.
3. Quoted in Teresa Hayter, *The Creation of World Poverty* (London: Pluto Press, 1981), p. 48.
4. Ibid.
5. Susan George, *How the Other Half Dies: The Real Reasons for World Hunger* (London: Penguin Books, 1976), p. 125.
6. Interview with Andrew Weil, head of Warren Weil Public Relations, autumn 1981, New York.
7. Ibid.
8. *Voice of Women*, July 1982.
9. Fuentes and Ehrenreich, p. 9.
10. Compiled from sources mentioned in note 2 above.
11. Fuentes and Ehrenreich, p. 23.
12. Ibid.
13. Ibid., p. 43.
14. See especially Hein Marais's coverage of 1989 AMRX, "War in Store", *Now*, June 1-7, 1989; and the work of Ernie Regher, Project Ploughshares, Kitchener-Waterloo, Ont.
15. Both Hayter and George advance this view.
16. Interview with Curtis Hoxtar, president of Hoxtar Public Relations, autumn 1981, New York.
17. Interview with Harold Burson, president of Burson Marsteller, autumn 1981, New York.
18. "The Electronics Industry", *Canada Asia Currents*, February 1981.
19. *British Companies Operating in the Philippines* (London: Catholic Institute for International Relations, 1984).

20. McKeen, p. 50.
21. Ronald Reagan, State of the Union Message, 1983.
22. Quoted in Stuart M. Butler, *Enterprise Zones: Pioneering in the Inner City* (Washington: The Heritage Foundation, 1980), p. 22.
23. Quoted in ibid., p. 23.
24. Quoted in Stuart M. Butler, *The Issue Bulletin*, The Heritage Foundation, July 10, 1980.
25. Quoted in Stuart M. Butler, "Enterprise Zones in Britain: The Experiment Begins", *The International Briefing*, The Heritage Foundation, June 21, 1981.
26. Ibid.
27. Jeffrey Simpson, "Recession Exacts Heavy Toll in Regional Economics", *The Globe and Mail*, May 3, 1982, p. R4; see also Tom Forester, *High-Tech Society* (Cambridge, Mass.: MIT Press, 1987), p. 12.
28. Anthony Moreton, "Region Aid Cuts Create Greatest Upheaval Since the '40s", *The Globe and Mail*, May 6, 1985, p. R7.
29. Edward Greenspon, "Thatcher's Economic 'Miracle' Begins to Lose Lustre", *The Globe and Mail*, May 2, 1989, p. A12.
30. Forester, pp. 245-247.
31. "Industry in Britain: The Government's Enterprise Strategy", *Survey of Current Affairs*, February 1988.
32. Jeremy Rifkin, *Algeny: A New Word – a New World* (New York: Penguin Books, 1984), p. 22.
33. "Industry in Britain".
34. Mulroney's cuts to post-secondary educational institutions are also intended to increase reliance on corporate input regarding funding for research programs.
35. Butler, *Enterprise Zones*, p. 25.
36. Shipping, *The Globe and Mail*, February 15, 1982, p. B13.
37. Ibid.
38. Michael Lynk, "Labour Law Erosion", in *The Facts on Free Trade*, ed. Ed Finn (Ottawa: CUPE, 1988), p. 75.
39. Telephone interview with Stephen Glaude, April 1989, Toronto.
40. Stuart M. Butler, "Enterprise Zones at Last May Be Ready to Combat Urban Decay", *Executive Memorandum*, The Heritage Foundation, March 31, 1989.
41. McKeen, p. 58.
42. Ibid., p. 56.
43. Quoted in *The Chronicle Herald*, March 1, 1989.
44. McKeen, p. 60.
45. Maduro, pp. 53-54.
46. Lynk, p. 77.
47. "Throne Speech Excerpts", *The Globe and Mail*, April 5, 1989.
48. Forester, pp. 50-80; the pollution in Silicon Valley is so high that studies have found miscarriages running at twice the normal rate for the nation and birth defects three times as prevalent. Soil and water contamination in the area is extensive, and nine tons of "reactive organic gases" are released into the air daily.

6. The "Greening" of Establishment PR

1. Interview with Jerry Wattel, president of Hill and Knowlton, autumn 1981, New York.
2. Quoted in Max Boas and Steve Chain, *Big Mac: The Unauthorized Story of McDonald's* (New York: New American Library, 1976), p. 16.

3. See Andre Carothers, "A Nation Drunk on Oil", *Greenpeace*, July-August 1989, p. 2; and the editorial "Black Spring", *The Village Voice*, April 18, 1989, p. 3.

4. Gail Richardson, "From the Editor", *Probe Post*, spring 1989, p. 5.

5. Stephen Duncan, "Environmentalists Are Beating Politicians at Their Own Game", *The Financial Post*, June 19, 1989, p. 14.

6. Cited in Michael Brown, *Laying Waste: The Poisoning of America by Toxic Chemicals* (New York: Pocket Books, 1979), p. 100.

7. Michael Brown, "A Toxic Ghost Town", *The Atlantic*, July 1989, p. 26.

8. Cited by Morris Wolfe in an interview, autumn 1981, Toronto.

9. Kalevi Poeg, "Money Talks", *Adbusters*, summer 1989, p. 55.

10. Quoted in ibid.

11. Kalle Lasn and Bill Schmalz, "Forests Forever?", *Adbusters*, summer 1989, p. 8.

12. Ibid.

13. Quoted in Mark Rogers, "Interference! CRTC Muzzles Campus & Community Radio", *Fuse*, April-May 1989, p. 7.

14. Quoted in ibid., p. 8.

15. Ibid.

16. John Massey, "Weasel Words", *Adbusters*, summer 1989, p. 49.

17. See Joyce Nelson, "Canada Dry: Pipedreams and Freshwater Politics", *This Magazine*, October 1987, pp. 12-18.

18. Tom Spears, "Scenery? We'll Paint Our Waste Firm Says", *The Toronto Star*, May 31, 1989, p. A20.

19. Quoted in Tim Tiner, "Pulling of Program Casts Nuclear Fears", *Now*, April 6-12, 1989, p. 13.

20. Quoted in ibid.

21. Ibid.

22. Quoted in David Crane, "Nuclear Fusion May Save Ozone, Scientist Says", *The Toronto Star*, February 1, 1989, p. A12.

23. Quoted in ibid.

24. Quoted in Derek Ferguson, "Nuclear Electricity Cheaper Than Coal, Inquiry Panel Agrees", *The Toronto Star*, April 5, 1989.

25. Richard Mackie, "$900 Million Is Added to Cost of Darlington Nuclear Station", *The Globe and Mail*, June 2, 1989, p. A15.

26. Mary Gooderham, "Popularity of Nuclear Power Ready to Rebound, Backers Predict", *The Globe and Mail*, June 8, 1989, p. A17.

27. Kenneth Brower, "The Destruction of Dolphins", *The Atlantic*, July 1989, p. 38.

28. Quoted in Lynda Hurst, "The Diapers Did Him In", *The Toronto Star*, July 8, 1989.

29. Paul Rauber, "With Friends Like These ...", *Mother Jones*, November 1986, pp. 37 and 47.

30. Kirkpatrick Sale, "The Forest for the Trees: Can Today's Environmentalists Tell the Difference?", *Mother Jones*, November 1986, pp. 25-33.

31. The World Commission on Environment and Development, *Our Common Future* (Oxford and New York: Oxford University Press, 1987).

32. Teresa Hayter, *The Creation of World Poverty* (London: Pluto Press, 1981).

33. Ibid., p. 15.

34. Ibid., p. 9.

35. *Our Common Future*, p. 89.

36. Ibid., p. 9 (my emphasis).

37. Ibid., p. 147.

38. Ibid., p. 1.

39. Ibid., p. 60.

40. Ibid., p. 8.
41. Ibid., pp. 277-278.
42. Ibid., pp. 16 and 86.
43. Ibid., p. 86.
44. Ibid., p. 46.
45. Ibid., p. 45.
46. Ibid., p. 126.
47. Ibid., p. 135.
48. Ibid., p. 209.
49. Ibid., p. 28.
50. Ibid., p. 13.
51. *Probe Post*, winter 1989, p. 21.
52. *Our Common Future*, p. 1.
53. *Probe Post*, winter 1989, pp. 24-25.
54. Craig McInnes, "Activists Hoping Summit Communique More Than 'Green Veneer'", *The Globe and Mail*, July 18, 1989, p. A11.
55. Quoted in ibid.
56. Ibid.
57. *Our Common Future*, p. 193.
58. Quoted in McInnes.
59. *Our Common Future*, pp. 45-46.
60. Ibid., p. 45 (my emphasis).

7. Triage: A Brief Conclusion

1. Marc H. Ellis, *Faithfulness in an Age of Holocaust* (Warwick, N.Y.: Amity House, 1986), p. 7.
2. Michael Brown, *Laying Waste: The Poisoning of America by Toxic Chemicals* (New York: Pocket Books, 1979), pp. 334-335.
3. Quoted in ibid., p. 335.
4. Ibid., p. 336.
5. Anastasia Toufexis, "Panic Over Power Lines", *Time*, July 17, 1989, p. 55. For a more detailed discussion of the issues, see Robert O. Becker, M.D., and Gary Selden, *The Body Electric: Electromagnetism and the Foundation of Life* (New York: William Morrow, 1985).
6. Paul Brodeur, "Annals of Radiation: The Hazards of Electromagnetic Fields", parts 1-3, *The New Yorker*, June 12, 19, and 26, 1989.